Dr Colin Morris is a renowned
ordained Methodist minister who served as ̶ ̶ ̶
Africa from 1956 to 1970, he was involved in the freedom struggle and
became the first President of the United Church of Zambia. On his
return to Britain, he was appointed General Secretary of the Methodist
Missionary Society and then elected President of the Methodist
Church. In 1978 he joined the BBC as Head of Religious Broadcasting
and afterwards became the BBC Controller for Northern Ireland.
He was the first presenter of the BBC religious documentary series
Everyman, has presented BBC Radio 4's *Sunday* programme and
regularly contributes to 'Thought for the Day'. He has written a
number of books, four of them with the former President of Zambia,
Kenneth Kaunda.

In happy memory of
Whit Foy,
preacher and prophet

BIBLE REFLECTIONS ROUND THE CHRISTIAN YEAR

Colin Morris

First published in Great Britain in 2005

Society for Promoting Christian Knowledge
36 Causton Street
London SW1P 4ST

British Library Cataloguing-in-Publication Data
A catalogue record for this book is available from the British Library

ISBN 0–281–05763–X

1 3 5 7 9 10 8 6 4 2

Designed and typeset by Kenneth Burnley, Wirral, Cheshire
Printed in Great Britain by Ashford Colour Press

Contents

Contents

Contents

Introduction

Let me come clean at the outset. I am a preacher, not a biblical scholar. I know there are well-blessed Christians who are both, but I'm not one of them. Confronted with a biblical passage which grips me as a subject for reflection, I wrestle with the best commentaries to ensure that I am not doing violence to either text or context, but then the communicator in me takes over. How can I make that theme come alive to a particular group of twenty-first-century Christians in a particular place at a particular time?

Like many preachers, I have hobby horses I mount at the slightest provocation – favourite texts, doctrines to which I revert again and again, themes that reinforce my personal faith. Understandably, evangelicals tend to be drawn to the cross, charismatics to Pentecost, liberals to the teaching of Jesus, catholics to the great passages of Christ-mysticism. The temptation is always to use a metaphorical magnifying glass and bring the light of the gospel to a burning focus on one or two doctrines rather than let the full spectrum of the historic faith cast its range of colours across our life and witness as though through a stained-glass window.

This is why the liturgical year imposes such a godly discipline on us: because it confronts us with every aspect of the Jesus event. It is often said that Christianity is an historical religion, not taken up with airy fantasies but anchored in facts hard enough to stub your toe on. It is a pyramid poised on a point, a stretch of time identified in the Apostles' Creed as 'Under Pontius Pilate'. That phrase survives not because the early Church wished to vilify an inconsequential Roman governor, but to earth ultimate religious truth in a particular period and place. It is one thing – as mythology does – to talk about virgins giving birth to holy children or gods dying and rising from the dead in a realm beyond time, quite another to slot the Jesus event into a calendar that scholars can check using their own tools.

So Christianity deals in facts; but as the liturgical year teaches us, if the gospel is to be heard in its fullness, all the facts must be deployed, not just a selection that suits our temperament or churchmanship. We would not be human if we did not look forward with relish to particular festivals such as Christmas or Easter or Pentecost; a rich blend of memory and experience renders them precious to us. But we must not linger overlong. As the men said to the disciples who stood paralysed by the ascension of Christ, 'Why do you stand gazing into heaven?' So they came back down to earth, returned to Jerusalem and got on with the job. The liturgical year moves us on so that we can reflect on Christ in all his offices.

A word about translations. Like many preachers I am quite promiscuous in my use of versions of the Bible. I find that an unfamiliar rendering of a well-known verse may shed fresh light on the subject. I hope it is not sexist to confess that I am particularly partial to one-man translations such as Moffatt, Weymouth and Ronald Knox because they were also preachers – members of the same trade union, as it were.

The discipline of writing this book has done my faith good, and I am very grateful to Ruth McCurry of SPCK for suggesting the theme and helping me to impose some structure on it. Like the best editors, she combines charm and ruthlessness in equal measure. I should acknowledge that several of these pieces began life in briefer form in the 'Thought for the Day' slot and I thank the BBC for allowing me to reproduce them.

ADVENT

I am Alpha and Omega: the beginning and the end

Revelation 1.8

The Christian year begins with the End. Advent anticipates the events that unfold from Christmas – the earthly life of the one who became recognized by his followers as the Messiah. But that's only half the story; the other half is less often preached about in Advent because it somehow seems alien and mysterious. This is the theme commonly called the Second Advent, the return of our Lord in glory to bring the present age to an end and to inaugurate a new one.

We cannot afford to neglect this doctrine because it states the majestic truth that what God started at the Creation and reaffirmed through the Incarnation he will finish at the Consummation. History won't drift on; it will be transformed by a decisive divine intervention.

Eschatology is the jaw-breaking name we give to those aspects of faith concerned with the end of the world. And Christianity shares a number of aspects of eschatology with other religions. The Greeks believed in immortality long before Christ; the Resurrection of the Body and the Last Judgement were central Jewish beliefs. Warnings about the end of the world are to be found in a number of religions. Zoroaster, the Arian prophet of Persia, preached that good and evil will clash decisively once and for all to bring the drama of history to a climax.

But one doctrine of last things is wholly original to Christianity, that of the *parousia* – the glorious return of Christ to inaugurate a new order. The Greek word refers to a monarch visiting one of his foreign embassies. There is disagreement among scholars about whether Jesus himself ever taught this, but certainly the early Church believed it – indeed, there is an account in the New Testament of Thessalonian Christians neglecting their work and standing around in the street, their heads craned upwards, looking anxiously for Christ's descent from the sky.

Believers cannot recite the Apostles' Creed, sing Advent hymns or read whole sections of the New Testament without realizing that they share common cause with some strange sects and individuals for whom the victory of God's kingdom is an imminent possibility rather than a remote ideal. God, they say, will bring history to a climax in a quite original way by revisiting the world, this time not incognito in Jesus of Nazareth but in such a form that every eye will see him.

This image of Christ returning in glory represents a truth for which words are totally inadequate. We are creatures of time and history. We have no mental or spiritual apparatus for imagining or expressing something that happens *to* history rather than *in* history. How can we get our minds around a reality that does not merely break through the barrier between time and eternity but actually abolishes it?

Hence, the wild visions and bizarre imagery of the book of Revelation, as the writer struggled to imagine what the End will be like. Obviously, it hadn't yet happened, so he couldn't have been an eye-witness. But the same might be said about the Creation. How could the writers of Genesis possibly know what happened at the beginning of all things? They weren't there.

Take a clue from the most popular of all forms of fiction, the detective novel. In every good detective novel there is a chapter fairly near the end when the character of the villain undergoes a subtle transformation. He says or does something which reveals that he isn't what he seems to be. Then having nailed down the villain's character, the author writes backwards from that chapter to the crime and forwards to its solution.

The authors of the biblical books, like detective story writers, took as their starting point not a series of events but a character. They concentrated on the creator, of whom they had personal knowledge, rather than upon the moment of creation, of which they had none. And they must have asked themselves: how would the God we know now have acted then? Just to be absolutely sure, they offered two accounts of the Creation which differ in detail but each is recognizably the self-disclosure of divine love.

2

Once the character of God was clear in their minds from personal experience, they could write backwards and forwards, confident that God's nature is and will remain consistent. 'Shall not the Judge of all the earth do right?' asks Abraham, bargaining with God for the citizens of Sodom and Gomorrah, appealing to moral constancy at the heart of the universe. Much later, the author of the epistle to the Hebrews gave that moral constancy a personal name – 'Jesus Christ, the same yesterday, today and for ever.'

If the creation story speaks of order, trust and love at the very beginning, it is because the Hebrew writers had found God in their own experience to be trustworthy, consistent and loving. And it is the God of whom we have knowledge now who will deal with us at the End.

Our fathers told us what you did in their time

Psalm 44.1

It a besetting sin of the believer to suffer bouts of religious nostalgia, looking back longingly at the 'good old days'. It is reassuring to realize that even the psalmist was occasionally overtaken by the same malaise. In churlish mood he complains to God that from what his fathers had told him, in their day the Almighty was much more decisive: he drove out the heathen with his strong arm. Now the godless seemed to have the upper hand; they were thriving. It was all so unfair.

This is one reason why the doctrine of Christ's return is important – it strikes at the root of religious nostalgia. Like the psalmist, the tougher the times in which we live, the more we are prone to look back and locate a Golden Age in the past. How we sometimes sigh for those long-lost days when all the church pews were full and Christianity was a power in the land!

The disciples, conscious of the former glory of their nation, asked, 'Lord, will you restore the Kingdom to Israel?' That's what we ask too – 'Lord, will you restore to the Methodists or the Anglicans or Presbyterians their former glory?' And we get a dusty answer, 'Behold, I am doing a new thing.'

It is always a danger sign when believers talk about calling the nation or the Church back to God. There is no way back to God. We could organize a sort of spiritual holiday tour of all the places where there were historic meetings with God – the vicinity of the burning bush where Moses encountered him; the Damascus road on which Paul met Christ; Luther's fortress-church at Wittenberg; Aldersgate Street where John Wesley was converted – but at any one of these places we might turn a corner and be confronted, as were Mary of Magdala and Salome on the morning of the resurrection, with an angel in white robes saying, 'He is not here; he's gone ahead of you!' There is no way back to God, only a way forward to him.

Now it is this salutary lesson that the Second Advent teaches the Church. It keeps the head of the ship of faith pointing into the wind, and puts its destiny in a true perspective. The Church has a secret history known only to God; its members are the worst judges of its health. We cannot assess the Church's true state by membership statistics, its financial balance sheet or the condition of its buildings.

There have been historical periods when the Church has been aglow with power and influence, but beneath her splendid outward aspect her heart has been almost dead and shrivelled. At other times, the Church has been laid waste, her buildings in ruins, her priests dead or in hiding, and yet in upper rooms and dark cellars men and women have gathered in secret to pore over the Bible and break bread and proclaim in a whisper the Lord's death until he comes. And a great new age was about to dawn.

Are we any nearer the full realization of the kingdom now than the first Christians were, or than believers of our parents' generation were? Who can say? This is the secret. The history of the Church has not been a triumphal progression from glory to glory, but a strange, broken, episodic story of death and resurrection; of decay and renewal; of sudden ends and strange new beginnings. There is a Cinderella-like quality to the Church. There she is, tattered and grubby among the pots and pans, and only to the eye of faith can it be seen that beneath the rags she is adorned as a bride for her husband. But that lies ahead, and we must keep looking toward the horizon, for it is from the beyond that the glorified Christ comes to meet us.

I sleep but my heart is awake

Song of Solomon 5.2

In Advent, we celebrate what has happened and live with an impending sense of what is about to happen, trying to cope with that dual time-scale expressed in Jesus' words: 'the time cometh and now is'. We are poised, as the New Testament says, 'in the time between the times', but 'already tasting the powers of the age to come'.

But it isn't possible to live indefinitely on a knife-edge of breathless expectancy, with bags mentally packed, expecting the Lord at any moment. No matter how fervently we take to heart Christ's warning that we must stay awake and watch, we inevitably revert to normality, as in the days of Noah, eating and drinking, marrying and giving in marriage. How could it be otherwise? We would go mad if we had to live for every minute of our days at the level of spiritual and psychological intensity appropriate to an ultimate crisis.

Jesus highlights this very problem by the story he tells of the bridegroom whose coming is delayed. The image of the bridegroom is a common one in the Bible. In the Old Testament, God is described as Israel's bridegroom, and in the New Testament, the Church is portrayed as the bride of Christ. But the fascinating thing about this parable of the bridegroom is that nowhere in it is there any mention of a bride. We must presume that the ten virgins, five wise and five foolish, represent the Church at its best and worst.

The parable suggests that Christ returns as an Eastern bridegroom who according to custom sets off with his friends to collect the bride from her parents' home, and the procession between the two houses is an occasion for jocularity and singing which carries on the still night air for long distances. He finally arrives at midnight. To those waiting, it looked as though he would never come, and so they fell asleep.

How, then, are we to combat our all-too-human frailty, our failure in expectation? We are offered a clue by a verse in the Song of Solomon, 'I sleep but my heart is awake.' Any mother knows exactly what that means. Sometimes she falls asleep exhausted beside her child; but no matter how deep her sleep, should the child stir, she is alert immediately. She lives on two different levels. We all do. Much of the routine of our lives, from eating a meal to riding a bicycle, we do almost without thinking so that we can give our minds to other things, but if anything unexpected happens we snap into instant attention.

The psychologist William James was once asked whether he believed in God, and he answered that he wasn't sure, but the issue seemed to him like a ticking clock in the room in which he worked. He was quite unaware of it until it stopped, and then he heard a strange silence. So he thought there was something at the back of his life of which he was outwardly heedless but inwardly aware. At the deepest levels of our being there is something in us which resonates to the voice of God as instinctively as a flower turns its face to the sun or a divining rod quivers in the presence of water in the desert.

We nourish this inner vigilance by those disciplines of religion we go through almost as a matter of routine: the half-remembered phrases of a thousand prayers; the rich imagery of many hymns; sermons galore that seem to have passed in through one ear and out at the other with the occasional illustration sticking in our memories; snatches of familiar Bible passages. They sink deep into our psyche but are capable of being triggered by the distant sounds of our approaching destiny. They help to keep the heart awake and alert for the bridegroom's approach.

The mystery was made known to me by revelation

Ephesians 3.3

Was St Thomas Aquinas joking when he once wrote that God had to reveal the truth of the gospel to us because we have neither the time nor the wit to find it out for ourselves? And C. S. Lewis said that he came to believe Christianity was true because it is a religion we could not have guessed. It had, he said, just that strange twist about it that real things have.

Well, how would we expect revealed truth as opposed to any other to present itself to us? Certainly, it ought not to be something we could work out ourselves in the first place, otherwise it wouldn't need to be revealed. And there ought to be something mysterious about it. Only false prophets offer religious truths that make perfect sense, for these truths are human inventions and what we have invented we can fully explain. If Jesus really did think divine thoughts humanely rather than human thoughts divinely, they were bound to blow the minds of those who heard them for the first time.

And revealed truth is likely to cause uproar rather than invite ready acceptance because it is tailor-made not for our comfort or immediate happiness but for our ultimate good. The bearer of such truth is unlikely to be the most popular person in town because he or she invites us to consider a view of the universe where we do not occupy the central position. In this sense, God's truth, far from sounding like good news, may strike some people as very bad news indeed and stir up resistance and hatred.

Above all, the one who reveals God's truth will be a holy person, not necessarily pious in the conventional sense but one whose personality expresses something unmistakable about the divine life. His life and teaching must be all of a piece: a living demonstration of what he says. Baron von Hügel defined a saint as someone who embodies the 'Isness' of God rather than the 'Oughtness' of morality. To a unique degree, by everything he did and was and said, Jesus bodied forth God's reality.

And God's revelation is not confined to words – it could be an event whose nature exposes something about the meaning of all events, a happening in history which sums up what history is about. The Christian revelation is specific, it was done 'under Pontius Pilate', yet it is universal in expressing all that God has done and intends to do with his world; transcendent because its origins and destiny are beyond history; and it is dynamic. It mediates power as well as offering explanation. By these tests, Jesus fits the bill.

CHRISTMAS SEASON

The Word became flesh

John 1.14

The textbooks say that in Greek thought the term 'Word' means the controlling and organizing principle behind the world, that which holds everything together and gives it meaning. And in Hebrew thought 'Word' is shorthand for the way in which God acts. He speaks, and something is done. Nowhere in the Genesis account of creation is there any reference to God doing anything; he merely spoke and things happened – 'And God said, "Let there be Light", and there was light.' Indeed, the prophet Isaiah declared that God created the universe out of the breath he expelled when he spoke. Hence, if you add Greek and Hebrew ideas together, that term 'Word' refers to all we can know of God through his actions in history.

And 'flesh' – we all know what that means. It's the frail, wayward stuff that enshrines human personality, the embodiment of all our sorrows and joys, health and sickness, grandeur and misery. So we know what the terms 'Word' and 'flesh' mean; it is that verb 'became' which expresses the mystery not just of Advent but of the entire Christian faith.

By what strange chemistry can the essence of divinity materialize in a human frame? I don't know, and I have never met anyone who does. Mercifully, there are many things in this life one doesn't have to understand in order to benefit from them. We can be sustained, comforted and changed by truth too deep to be fathomed by the human mind.

This is God speaking to us in a language we understand. How does God communicate with us? Some religions say: through the spirits that inhabit the natural world, rivers and rocks and mountains. One religion says: through an infallible book that dropped from heaven into the lap of the founder;

others swear by astrology – the truth sketched out in the conformation of the stars. Christianity claims that the Word became flesh. God speaks through the truth taking possession of a human personality.

This is how most of the truth that really matters comes to us – not through abstract propositions or theories but through the agency of human encounter. Here is an orphan. He will get precious little comfort from a manual on child care: he needs a mother. A medical dictionary is no cure for the seriously sick; they need the healing touch of doctor or nurse. And no doctrine of salvation can release someone imprisoned in a private hell. They need a saviour: truth personalized, the Word become flesh.

And the Word became flesh to bind God and this world together. Word and flesh: God and the world. You can't have one without the other. You can't choose God and write the world off as irrelevant as some pietists seek to do, nor try to remake the world without taking account of God – which is the error of the idealist. If you want one, you must have the other. God without the world is an enigmatic abstraction; the world without God is a terrifying fiction.

Who does this world belong to? Some misguided believers say: to the Devil, keep clear of it. Others say, from their reading of history, that it belongs to whoever is strong enough to dominate it, so accept the inevitable. The New Testament says the world belongs to God, so go in there and claim it for him.

If we have any doubt about where to find God, because the Word became flesh we must go to wherever flesh is being tortured and broken and imprisoned and starved, and there we will find Christ.

Where else might we find him? In a magnificent cathedral, venerable parish church, tin-roofed mission hall? Yes, on one condition: that the Word becomes flesh there. If the Word is transmuted into majestic architecture, glorious music and eloquent liturgy but does not become flesh; if our prayers remain pious words and don't become flesh in sacrificial service in God's world, then we are putting the Incarnation into reverse, spiritualizing it.

The Word also became flesh to express an extraordinary truth – not our dependence upon God, but God's dependence upon us. The Word, almighty, irresistible power, becomes frail, weak flesh to symbolize the truth that God puts himself at our mercy. What could be more dependent than a baby? In its help-lessness is prefigured the strategy of the cross where God saves us not by a demonstration of divine might but earthly impo-tence; ultimate power expressed through powerlessness.

Didn't Jesus need a human womb from which to be born; a human breast at which to suck; a father to carry him away to Egypt away from Herod's wrath; a group of friends to support and eventually to betray him; a conscript to carry his cross? Is it not true today? Does not God need human hands to wield the instruments through which he heals; a human voice to bring comfort to the distressed and distress to the comfortable; human brain power to help make deserts fertile and feed the hungry; human political skills dedicated to creating a more just and humane social order?

The Word become flesh is a tremendous demonstration of faith – not our faith in God, that flickers and fades, waxes and wanes, but God's faith in us, entrusting himself and the fate of his kingdom into our shaky hands.

Thou hast put joy and gladness in my heart (Boxing Day)

Psalm 4.7

Boxing Day is so called because it was the day when priests distributed the money emptied out of the church poor box on Christmas Day. So it started off as the very poor persons' Christmas. Then the wealthy took the day over and in the nine-teenth century it became a bank holiday – one of those days when the banks are shut. Yet the word 'holiday' still means a holy day. So a bank holiday could be thought of as a holy day for bank employees.

Now the old religious holidays were marked by all kinds of rituals. So by what rituals might bankers celebrate their holy day? Do they dance around bonfires made up of burning ledgers? They could take a leaf out of the book of the great religions; for instance, they might copy that ancient Festival of Jubilees celebrated by the Jews of the Old Testament when every seventh year all property had to be returned to its original owners and all debts forgiven. How's that for an enlightened banking policy? Bankers' children could leave standing orders at the foot of their beds for Santa to fill in. The directors of the big banks might emulate one of the Shinto festivals, cover themselves in sackcloth and ashes and solemnly recite the names of all the dud companies they have loaned our money to in the past year. Bank employees could process through the streets and read poetry in honour of their founders, rather as Muslims do on the birthday of the Prophet.

Though the modern bank holiday has no religious origin, it still has religious sanction. For any holiday hints at the answer to that big question posed by much recent scientific argument about the origin of the universe. The really big question is not, 'How did the universe come into being?' but 'Why?' And according to one theological tradition, God created the universe just for fun. The argument runs: the Creation can't have been essential to God. If he had to make it, then he wasn't a free agent; he was acting under a necessity which was more powerful than he is, so he would be less than God. Therefore he made the universe for his own goodwill and pleasure.

Great festivals were meant to put us in touch with the joy at the heart of things. Christianity does not nullify the festive jollity; it provides a compelling reason for it.

Call his name Jesus

Matthew 1.23

It often comes as a shock to pious Northern Protestants to visit Catholic countries and find many males named Jesus. It is much easier to believe in a God-like being called Christ imprisoned in the Authorized Version than it is in a Messiah called Jack or its first-century equivalent, Jesus, who lived in the next hovel, drank at the same well and used the same outside privy. William

Temple in one of his best-known aphorisms declared that Christianity is the most materialistic of all the great religions. The Christian faith doesn't blush at our carnality. It is not disconcerted by all the evidences of mortality. If the Word really became flesh, it assumed not just the noblest but also the most elemental of human functions, some of which are undignified to the point of ludicrousness. It may not be good taste to spell them out but it is sound theology to insist that unless we can give full weight to the word 'flesh' in the most basic as well as exalted sense, the Incarnation was a sham. As it says in the letter to the Hebrews, 'Jesus was tempted at all points as we are.' And that would not be possible unless he were fully human.

As soon as we learn our own names we tend to assume they label us as unique, different from anybody else in the whole world; then we slowly discover we're just one of a number who share our name. In Britain, if you wanted to give your child a unique name, you could call him Jesus, whereas not only in Latin countries but also in biblical times Jesus was a very popular name. There were many people around Palestine called Jesus or at least the Hebrew original, Joshua. There was nothing special about the name; it was just the first-century equivalent of, say, Jack. But what a different slant it would have put on Christianity if the Bible translators, instead of replacing that Hebrew name Joshua with the Greek name Jesus had gone the whole hog and given him a good English name like, say, Jack.

Think of all those hymns that make great play of the sacredness of the name Jesus – we would end up singing verses like 'How sweet the name of Jack sounds' or 'Jack shall reign where'er the sun', or reciting in the Creed, 'I believe in God the Father Almighty and in Jack his only son our Lord.' Hymn words can become so familiar that we barely register their meaning, but if to us the replacement of Jesus by Jack sounds blasphemous, to the Jewish people of the first century it would be the height of absurdity to treat the name Jesus with special reverence.

Could the lad next door called Jack really be the Messiah? The Gospels are shot through with references to people wondering whether this one or that one might be the Messiah. No one seemed to be sure.

Two thousand years on, some Christians are incredulous that Jesus' contemporaries did not recognize him as the Messiah, though he didn't go out of his way to make it plain. We, of course, would have had no doubt about his identity – or would we? We might admit that had we been in Jerusalem on a certain day, we wouldn't find much to choose between an unpleasant nationalist whose name was Barabbas and an enigma who, as the prophet Isaiah predicted, was destined to be despised and rejected by his contemporaries.

We might ponder the fact that our own record as Messiah-spotters is uneven: 'Lord, when did we see you hungry or naked or sick or in prison?' Oh, there are so many Toms, Dicks and Harrys fallen on hard times that we barely notice them, but if someone special like Jesus crossed our path in distress, then we would rush to his aid. Or would we?

This is precisely the point Jesus was making in the parable of the sheep and the goats. We would expect to be in awe of God in heaven, but it is the God next door who demands our response in this Christmas season.

Are you the one we are expecting or should we look elsewhere?

Matthew 11.3

For the first five centuries of Christian history there was no Christmas Day. The Church felt no need to assign a fictitious date to Christ's birth because whenever they met, every week in fact, the early Christians celebrated Christmas and Easter.

I suspect that if the Church proposed that our society revert to the original Christmas idea, the general public wouldn't stand for it. They would fight to the last drop of sherry and the penultimate mince pie to ensure that their annual bout of winter roistering continue. And why not? The modern Christmas is as much the invention of the Industrial Revolution as the steam engine is, so it makes no more sense to bellyache about the commercialization of Christmas than to bemoan the wet-ness of water.

The point is, this top-dressing of religion that our society still clings to at Christmas – the crib and manger and shepherds and all that – is a charming but minor aspect of its meaning. Christmas is really about the arrival of the Messiah, and there's an incident in Matthew's Gospel where the disciples of John the Baptist enquire of Jesus whether he is the Messiah. They ask, 'Are you the one we're expecting or should we look for another?' The interesting thing is that in his reply, Jesus doesn't mention a star or stable or shepherds or wise men. Instead, he says, 'Tell John that the blind see, the lame walk, the deaf hear, the poor have some good news.' In other words, tell John the revolution has started.

That's the idea behind Christmas. Jesus' reply to the dis-ciples of John puts Christmas into an entirely different context from jolly festivity and all that. He is saying in effect that the Messiah confronts our society more as Menace than Merry-maker. John Donne, perhaps the most famous Dean of St Paul's, once wrote, 'I need thy thunder O God, thy songs no longer suffice me.' The Messiah doesn't gurgle at us out of a crib but towers over us, posing a threat to a lifestyle we cherish. He's going to turn things upside down; or rather, set them the right way up, by taking away from us what we ought never to have had and giving us what we might not want but desperately need – salvation, not as superheated pietism but as the justice, peace and joy of the kingdom.

The Messiah is destined to establish his reign upon the earth, and sooner or later he's going to pitch up on our doorstep. That's the Christmas Idea and there's no escaping it.

EPIPHANY SEASON

There came wise men from the East

Matthew 2.1

Epiphany traditionally marks the showing forth of Christ to the Gentiles in the incident of the wise men paying homage to the infant Jesus. It is a story which was rich in symbolism for early Christians – the King of the Jews was to be the universal Lord, and the death of Jesus spelt the end of the hereditary principle. The boast was once, 'We are children of Abraham', but the gospel insists that the key to salvation rests not on lineal descent but on spiritual character. The Jewish rite of circumcision – a symbol of exclusiveness – could be replaced by baptism, proclaiming the nearness of all to God.

So in the visit of the Magi there is foreshadowed the spread of the gospel throughout the world. These wise men who shared a creed of venerable antiquity represented the first turning of the Gentile mind to Christ, acknowledging the existence of an even brighter star than they as astronomers had ever detected.

There are many historical problems about this account which is recorded only in Matthew's Gospel. Tradition has promoted the wise men from sages to kings; firmed up on the number, three; given them names, Caspar, Melchior and Balthasar, and identified their gifts as gold, frankincense and myrrh. And the Adoration of the Magi has provided classical religious art with one of its most popular and enduring subjects. In the Middle Ages they were venerated as the patron saints of travellers and inns, and the Milanese claim to possess their relics.

Yet deep beneath the layers of tradition, there is the bedrock truth which the Magi symbolize – not just the opening of the whole geographical world to the gospel but also the intellectual world, for it was their astronomy, their science, their learning which brought them to Christ.

Throughout Christian history the human reason has been viewed in some circles with grave suspicion. The Bible itself seems to be in two minds on the matter. 'Can you by searching find out God?' asks Job, obviously expecting a negative answer, and yet Jesus said, 'Seek and you will find.' The book of Proverbs declares that wisdom is more precious than rubies, whereas Paul dismisses philosophy as a vain deceit and asks, 'Hasn't God made the wisdom of the world to appear foolish?' And yet . . . in a different mood, Paul urges Christians to pray with the Spirit and with understanding and tells them, 'In mind, be mature.'

We human beings are unique in having a thirst for explanation. We do not merely experience, we reflect; we don't just endure, we enquire. And we ask insistently, 'Why? What is it all about; how did it all begin; where will it all end?' We are driven to attempt to formulate theories about the world. And religion answers the human hunger for explanation by ascribing a meaning to life which may go far beyond the available evidence. It is a matter of faith, but it works for those who accept it as a source of inspiration and a means of support. When people say, 'I don't know what I'd do without my religion', they presumably mean it offers them a satisfying way of explaining the otherwise inexplicable, giving them the confidence that everything will be all right in the end, providing them with the strength to soldier on.

There are important limits to explanation. Christianity explains a lot but it does not make the mistake of trying to explain everything. It observes a proper reticence about the strictly mysterious element in life – not what is as yet unknown until the Big Brains get around to unravelling it, but what will remain for ever unknowable; mystery not to be found beyond the present frontiers of knowledge but existing at the heart of the simplest things and everyday experiences. It recognizes that we are dealing with one who is beyond the range of our senses, who comes to meet us out of dazzling darkness, only if and when he chooses.

The lesson of the appearance of the sages at Bethlehem is that God will guide whoever follows his star faithfully. He spoke to the wise men through a star, to Joseph by a dream, to the shepherds by an unearthly melody, to Simeon by an inner vision. 'We know in part,' said Paul, 'and we prophesy in part.' Or as Ephesians puts it, the gospel is 'knowledge in a mystery'. So the intellect can only take us so far. But we have got to go as far as it will take us. The Magi reached Bethlehem by a combination of scientific learning and religious longing.

Of those born of woman, there has risen none greater than John

Matthew 11.11

The story of Jesus' baptism by John is traditionally celebrated on this Sunday, so it is appropriate to compare and contrast these two prophets of Israel.

Throughout a stormy history the people of Israel developed apocalyptic expectations. Surviving in the melting pot of the Near East, threatened by great empires such as Assyria, the Jews defiantly assured themselves and anyone else who would listen to them that God would not tolerate for ever their humiliation. Otherwise, they felt the Covenant they had concluded with Jehovah was worthless.

This hoped-for transformation of their fortunes sharpened into expectation of an event which they described as the Day of the Lord when the whole world would be forced to acknowledge their privileged status in the eyes of God, and recognize them as top-dog nation. But prophets such as Amos inveighed against the idea that God would allow himself to be used to glorify Israel without taking any account of their sinfulness: 'Woe unto you that desire the day of the Lord! It is darkness and not light. As if a man did flee from a lion and a bear met him; or went into a house and leaned his hand on the wall, and a serpent bit him. Shall not the Day of the Lord be darkness and not light?'

This strain runs throughout the prophetic tradition in the Old Testament, then there is a long silence until John the Baptist bursts upon the scene, proclaiming a menacing Day of the

Lord whose worst consequences could only be mitigated by a baptism of repentance. The old Judaism was finished, an axe was laid to the root of the tree, a furnace would burn up the chaff of Judaism with an unquenchable flame.

A whole era ended with John. He is reported as saying, 'I have baptized you with water but one comes after me who will baptize you with the Holy Spirit.' John's ministry marked the limit set on the upward movement of Old Testament Judaism. It went far and achieved much. It was full of heroic possibilities and stirred high hopes, but it pointed towards a fulfilment that was beyond its own powers. This is why the fourth Gospel is much concerned with the contrast between John the Baptist and Jesus. To the outward eye they are alike; inwardly they are poles apart. Outwardly, they seem to belong to one movement and preach the same kingdom. In reality, they stand on different planes and arrive on the stage of history from different directions. Referring to John the Baptist, the prologue of John's Gospel insists, 'He was not that Light.'

Jesus and John were also very different personality types. John was a strict ascetic living remote from society, not even dependent on it for his food. He bathed in cold water and followed a strict regime of fasting. He was of a gloomy and fearful disposition. It is impossible to imagine John the Baptist using a wedding feast as an image for what the Day of the Lord would be like.

When Jesus transferred his work to Galilee, he paid a great tribute to John but still abandoned John's chosen method of baptism. Paul summed up the difference between the stern John and the encouraging Jesus in the words, 'We did not receive the spirit of slavery, but a childlike spirit by which we cry, "Abba, dear father."'

The radical difference between John and Jesus is most marked in their teaching about the End, their message as prophets of judgement. John warned, 'The judgement of wrath is coming' whereas Jesus promised 'The kingdom of Heaven is at hand.' Luke's Gospel put it in a nutshell, 'The law and the prophets were until John; then the kingdom of God is preached.'

John the Baptist foretold the arrival of the kingdom; Jesus embodied it. For the early Christians, Jesus was the clue to the meaning of the kingdom, the only way in; the sole image by which it could be visualized. The gospel of Christ and the gospel of the kingdom meant the same thing because by his passion, death and resurrection, Christ embodied all that the kingdom symbolized. The kingdom is wherever he is, and to receive him gladly on his return is to secure eternal citizenship of it. That vision soared beyond the knowledge of the one whom Jesus praised as the greatest born of woman.

We do not yet see everything controlled by man but we do see Jesus

Hebrews 2.9

The philosopher and mathematician A. N. Whitehead wrote, 'I hazard a prophecy that that religion will conquer which can render clear to popular understanding some eternal greatness incarnate in the passage of temporal facts.' Well, here is a temporal fact with a vengeance. The link between God and the world is forged not through a philosophical idea or a code of morality but in a human life, that of the man Jesus.

Christianity is a religion based not on ideas or speculation but on facts; not on something thought but on something done; not on insubstantial dreams but on tangible realities – as the author of the Epistle of John put it: 'that which we have heard and seen with our eyes and *touched with our hands* concerning the words of life'.

Every human being is an embodied fact, and this one is also a decisive fact, as Simeon told Mary: 'This child is set for the fall and rising of many in Israel.' There are some facts which have only passing interest, and others which demand responses. 'Is that the Thames flowing at the bottom of your garden?' will elicit a polite reply, but 'The river flowing at the bottom of your garden is overflowing its banks' will produce instant action. Babies are bundles of imperious demands, they are very hard to ignore. In particular, they turn things upside down; within the reach of their tiny fists, they rearrange every-thing movable.

Someone has said, 'The best way to send an idea is to wrap it up in a person.' That's the theory behind Christmas: divine love wrapped up in a person, or as the carol puts it, 'Love came down at Christmas.'

Unlike philosophical principles, human beings occupy space; they are born and die at specific times. Theological doctrine and abstract ideas have no precise origin, but the birth of a human being is a tangible event; it can be traced to a specific time and place, during an historically confirmed census in the land of Judaea. It is an event scholars can corroborate. So be it. If the historical basis of the Christian faith can be undermined, it ought to be, for the claims it makes for this child are breathtaking.

The coming of Jesus was a prophetic fact – the beginning of the End in the sense that it pointed forward to a new order; indeed, he was the first and original embodiment of it. Once, we understood little about the laws that govern the universe, then along came Isaac Newton, a prophetic fact pointing to a whole new amazing scientific enlightenment. Once, there was little scientific medicine, then along came Pasteur and Lister – prophetic facts. The battle against disease is not yet over, we do not have final mastery; but thanks to the trailblazers we are on our way.

And the coming of Jesus is a profoundly influential fact in the sense that though vast impersonal forces seem for the most part to drive history, in the end it is by the quality of individu-als that things are changed decisively for the better. Sir Arthur Keith once claimed that if three hundred people were taken out of history we should still be living in the Stone Age. One might make the same point in reverse: add a handful of human beings of the Hitler breed and we could soon find ourselves living again in darkness.

There is one great difference between many forms of know-ledge such as science or philosophy and that offered by Jesus. Take Freud or Descartes or Einstein out of the picture and we might still have their ideas; their discoveries stand in their own light; others can reduplicate their thought processes or experi-ments. But you cannot have the gospel without Jesus, for the simple reason that love has no meaning in isolation from the lover; it doesn't linger on as an abstract quality, however noble. In the deepest realms of the moral life it is not possible to separate out principles and personality. Emerson said of the Roman orator Seneca, 'He had the most noble thoughts; if only he'd had the moral right to them.'

William James, the American psychologist, was asked to define holiness. He responded by pointing silently to Bishop Phillips Brooks. Christ himself is Christianity. He is the one persistent and eternal factor in the Christian faith. So the Incarnation means this: a personality has come into the world who does not merely point towards but embodies God's new creation.

The Greeks seek after wisdom

I Corinthians I.22

The Gentiles who encountered Jesus found a mind strange to them, one that did not conform to their understanding of a wise man. The man of Nazareth was no philosopher. The Greeks who went up to Jerusalem for the Passover and asked Philip to introduce them to Jesus would have been bitterly disappointed if they expected to meet a swarthy-faced Jewish Plato engaged in endless dialogue with his disciples about the nature of truth. Jesus was firmly within the Eastern tradition of the wandering guru who is not very talkative and speaks in riddles and stories intended to be passed on by word of mouth rather than through textbooks.

For two reasons, Jesus would not qualify as a philosopher. He had no interest in those speculative questions beloved of intellectuals. Musings such as 'Let us assume that . . .' or 'What would happen if . . .' did not pass his lips. He did not say, 'Let us ponder the conundrum of evil'; he said, 'A farmer planted a field and during the night his enemy came and sowed weeds in it.' He did not wrestle with metaphysical questions to do with the relationship between good and evil – he dispatched the issue with one sharp rhetorical question, 'Is it lawful on the Sabbath to do good or harm, to save life or to destroy it?'

The other reason Jesus would not qualify as a philosopher is that he was a man with a magnificent obsession. His spiritual and mental energies were not diffused to cast light across the widest possible area of ignorance but brought to a burning focus on one issue – the kingdom of God. This is the central theme of his parables; in its thought he lives and dies. The heretic Marcion was undoubtedly right when he commented that the kingdom of God is Jesus himself; he embodied it, to know him was to be confronted with God's kingly rule.

And yet, considering how majestic this concept of God's kingly rule is and how deep its roots are sunk in the history of the Jewish people, the teaching of Jesus about it is curiously parochial. He does not sketch out any blueprint of the New Jerusalem; he points to the Messianic secret hidden away in the concrete actualities of everyday life here and now rather than expressed in expansive philosophical principles about some ideal state.

Unlike many philosophers, Jesus was as much concerned with the 'How' of things as with the 'What' and 'Why' of them. When the rich young ruler asks him for counsel, Jesus doesn't debate eternal verities; he offers the severely practical advice, 'Sell all you have and give it to the poor.' There is a moral here for Christian leaders overwhelmed by the bureaucracy of religion and slowly sinking from sight under mountains of paper, who begrudge the time spent on the nuts and bolts of ecclesiastical business – the letters to be written, the committees to be attended, the meetings to be addressed, the reports to be read. We cry in outrage and despair, 'If only we hadn't this lot to cope with we could get on with the real job!'

But if Jesus teaches anything, it is that all too often *this* is the real job. The secret of the kingdom is hidden in the mechanics rather than the metaphysics of life – mundane matters distracting our attention from lofty contemplation of the riddle of the universe.

The mind of Christ, that's what you've got to develop, says Paul; a mind concentrated on specifics rather than darting hither and thither speculating about the 'just suppose thats' and 'if onlys' of existence. You must look for the secret of kingdom not hidden in the profound epigrams of the wisest sage you know but momentarily revealed in the eyes of the person next door.

The Christian as philosopher may roam at will throughout the universe of knowledge if he or she has the cast of mind and training, but the minds of disciples must be firmly earthed in the next routine chore, the next casual encounter, the next experience that comes along. The vague generalities of faith require a telescope; Jesus had microscopic vision, concentrated on the individual hairs of one's head or the single sparrow that falls to the ground. We shall rediscover the joy of our religion when we stop generalizing, turn away from the big maps and trace God in the little diary of our obscure life. The true disciple finds God in particular decisions.

They drew lots and the lot fell on Matthias

Acts 1.26

The French philosopher Pascal stated the case for God in the form of a wager. We must decide what our gains and losses would be if we were to stake everything on God's existence. If we win, we gain eternal life; if we lose, we lose nothing at all, since oblivion is the obvious alternative. If there is only one chance in a million of God existing, it is still better to stake everything on the remote possibility, because a finite loss is nothing compared to the chance of an infinite gain. So, asks Pascal, what have we to lose?

Choices can be momentous or trivial. I can choose to watch television or go out to the cinema; that's a trivial option because nothing much hangs on it. But if Christopher Columbus had said to me, 'Sail with me and we'll discover a whole new world!' and I decided to stay at home and tend my garden, the option I went for would be momentous and irreversible.

Jesus told a parable which made the same point. Some of those invited to the feast of the kingdom cried off, saying they had married a wife or bought some oxen or had to look over a property and couldn't attend – choices that seemed severely practical at the time but which proved to be of crucial significance.

It is rarely our minds which make these momentous choices between options. Every piece of evidence pointing to God's existence can be balanced by another casting doubt on it. The sceptic who says he hasn't got enough evidence to make up his mind is saying that his fear of being wrong is more important to him than his hope of being right. Putting it at its lowest, the philosopher William James said that religion is a hypothesis which might be true, and we have the right to believe it at our own risk. The most decisive way of refusing to believe something is to act as though it were untrue. If I'm not sure I can trust you, I will share nothing significant about myself with you, and practically, that is tantamount to distrusting you. If I refuse to lend a hand bailing out a sinking rowing boat because I doubt it is possible to keep it afloat, I'm actively helping to sink her. While I make up my mind, life has settled the issue. I may hold off making up my mind about the reality of God, but I cannot delay making up my life.

William James also formulated a rule about all this. He wrote, 'Always believe what is in line with your needs.' It sounds more like wishful thinking than a theological doctrine, but it's worth pondering. He offers the example of a man climbing a mountain who has got himself into such a position that he can only escape by a mighty leap across a crevasse. If he has faith that the leap is possible, he has already added to the probability he will succeed; if he trembles and doubts and hesitates, then launches himself in a moment of despair, he has already subtracted from his chances of success because his beliefs are in opposition to his needs.

So far as human beings stand for anything beyond the barest biological realities, they run the risk of being mistaken. All human creativity, enterprise and discovery begin with a brave 'Perhaps' and could end in a crashing 'No!' Just as the essence of courage is to stake one's life on a possibility, so the first step of faith is to accept the possibility that God exists.

After all, the first demand Jesus made on his disciples wasn't that they should worship him or think beautiful thoughts about him but that they should follow him – 'Do what I command' he said. Act like a Christian.

To act as if God exists is to pray as if there is someone who hears our prayers. It is to live as if we have been finally and fully forgiven for Jesus' sake; it is to love our neighbour as if God himself had commanded it, it is to live in the present as if we were destined to live for ever. That is how G. K. Chesterton became a Christian. Though prayer meant nothing to him personally, he took it up as a discipline because it meant a lot to godly people whose character and spirit he admired. He hoped that by living as if prayer worked, he might get the point. And he did.

EPIPHANY TO LENT: ORDINARY TIME

Therefore, God gave them up

Romans 1.24

The reality of divine judgement is central to any understanding of the gospel, and there are a number of interrelated strands on this theme to be found in the Bible. Take perhaps the most surprising. God's judgement in history seems to operate sometimes through inaction; God apparently doing absolutely nothing. The Old Testament prophets claimed that God sometimes pronounced judgement by allowing things to take their course. According to the prophet Jeremiah, God says, 'I will hide my face from them and then see what their end shall be' or 'Thy sins shall correct thee' – disaster resulting from God's non-intervention, his withdrawal from history. There are tiny but significant details in a couple of Jesus' parables. He talks about a man (and we are to understand he means God) who planted a vineyard and then went abroad. The owner absents himself, apparently leaving the tenants to wreak what havoc they will. In Paul's letter to the Romans there are some terrible words to this effect. Writing about one group of people, he comments, 'Therefore, God gave them up.' He didn't hurl thunderbolts at them or strike them down, he merely left them to their own devices.

One of the most striking features of the Gospels is how tight-lipped Jesus was. He certainly didn't nag people into the kingdom of heaven. 'Poor little talkative Christianity', sneered E. M. Forster. It didn't get the habit from its founder. His most powerful messages were wordless. He kept silent about his mission for thirty years; to this very day, no scholars are sure whether he did or did not claim to be the Messiah – 'Are you he that should come or do we wait for another?' asked the disciples

26

of John. The answer was equivocal. Jesus rarely answered a direct question, and his response to some incidents was silence. When he was told that John had been murdered he said nothing but went into the desert; when the Syro-Phoenician woman asked him to heal her daughter he didn't reply; and when the woman taken in adultery was brought to him in the midst of a great clamour, he said nothing and wrote in the sand. He made no attempt to defend himself before Caiaphas or Herod or Pilate. He exasperated them by his silences. It is as though Jesus was content to let things take their course because he had absolute trust in the moral order God had established for the world.

One of the most disturbing stories in the Gospel is that of the healing of the ten lepers. Jesus heals all ten; but only one, a Samaritan, returns to thank him. The other nine go their way and resume their old life. The interesting question is this: why did Jesus accept the situation without protest or complaint? Why didn't he call the nine back and remonstrate with them, pointing out what a miracle had been done for them and how they were insulting God by their ingratitude? No, he leaves it at that. He accepts their verdict.

The moral of the parable is that God in his own ways and times makes himself known to us. And if we are unmoved by him, the danger is not that in his anger he may consume us but that he may accept his failure without protest. By the rules he himself has laid down, we must be treated as mature, responsible individuals. We are given our chance, we make our choice, and God accepts it. In effect, we have judged him, and in the process we have been judged.

Inasmuch as you did it to the least of these, you did it to me

Matthew 25.40

One of the favourite themes of the New Testament writers is that of God breaking into our lives like a burglar. It occurs in Thessalonians, Peter and Revelation. And it is a very familiar preaching theme, especially when associated with the parable of the king going abroad to visit a far country, where it is made clear that this world is still the king's domain and all over it are reminders of his sovereignty in case we should forget and begin to imagine we own the place. He jolts us with reminders that he is the ruler still.

Where are these reminders? Everywhere: wherever there are sick to be healed, hungry to be fed, naked to be clothed, prisoners to be visited – for these are not just examples of God's less fortunate children; the Word has become flesh in them. We meet him in them; we reject him when we turn our backs on them.

The image of the Christ who sneaks back into history like a thief in the night well illustrates the balance that has to be struck in our thinking between recognizing that Christ is always encountering us surreptitiously and will also one day be manifest in glory; between acknowledging the Christ who as Spirit stirs our hearts now and the Christ who as King will shake the earth at the end.

And the image of the thief in the night draws dramatic attention to this dual timescale within which believers must live. This warning in the Gospel about Christ constantly encountering us is puzzling. For the most part, we aren't conscious that we are always bumping into the one who embodies our judgement. How are we to know? Jesus replies, 'Truly I tell you that what you did to the least of these, you did to me.' And then he catalogues the legion of the lost and lonely and outcast. That's how we know. The question is simply: did you or did you not answer the cry of distress of your neighbour, whether he or she lives next door or on the other side of the world? We are divinely judged by our answer to that question. Christ hidden in our neighbour, that's the standard.

The voice of almighty God in judgement is heard, not booming from beyond the stars, but in the cry of the hungry for bread, the downtrodden for dignity and the victim for justice. He keeps silent so that they can speak for him. That is a quite astonishing and frightening thought – the Eternal One who inhabits the Heaven of heavens and rides upon the whirlwind, before whom all the nations are as a drop in a bucket, says nothing so that you can hear the cry of the downtrodden. They speak for him. In their wail of anguish there is more divine judgement upon us than torrents of heavenly denunciation.

This is the judgement, that light has come into the world

John 3.19

There are two statements in John's Gospel which seem to be contradictory: 'I came not to judge the world but to save the world' but 'For judgement I came into the world.' How can these two statements be reconciled? The fourth Gospel does it through the image of Jesus as the Light of the world – 'This is the judgement, that light is come into the world and men love the darkness rather than light.' It's the notion of judgement almost as an inevitable by-product of Jesus' presence: judgement by exposure to the truth. We can get by in the semi-gloom with our deceptions, illusions and half-truths, until light comes into the world and we are ruthlessly unmasked.

H. E. Fosdick said sin is belatedness; it is being behind the times, clinging to ancient darkness after the light has come. Johann Sebastian Bach was forgotten for a hundred years after his death, but he shed a new light upon music that a century of neglect could not extinguish. Music could never be the same again. There was a time when we believed that the earth was flat, then the light came and flat-earthers were exposed as hopelessly outdated; once, slavery and child labour were the acceptable order of the day, then the light came and the use of human beings as things became an intolerable evil; once, the wreaking of vengeance to the third and fourth generation on those who had wronged us was regarded as the noblest of actions, then the light came – Jesus said, 'Love your enemies, do good to them that persecute you', and we had to face a new standard of judgement.

My first church after I left theological college was in the South Yorkshire coalfields and I had a landlady who was fiercely house-proud, as Yorkshire women often are. Every Monday she washed the sheets and there they flapped in the wind, their sparkling cleanliness not harmed by the fact that they had the pit slag-heap as a backdrop. Then one weekend it snowed and the slag-heaps were covered in blindingly white snow, and against that backdrop, my landlady's sheets looked just a little less pristine. Judgement by the light. I'm as good as the next person, unless the next person happens to be Jesus Christ.

He will have the world judged in righteousness by a man

Acts 17.31

Let's be honest, Jesus did not make it easy for us to decide what sort of a timescale we ought to have in mind for his glorious return. He was frankly equivocal. In one place he hints that it is rapidly approaching, 'Truly I say to you that this generation will not pass away but these things will be accomplished', or 'There are some of you here present who will not die until they have seen the Kingdom of God come in power.' Somewhere else he discerned it as a more distant prospect with an intervening period of gradual diffusion – 'first the blade then the ear then the full corn'; indeed, there are a number of parables such as the mustard seed and leaven where the establishment of the kingdom seems to be subject to the laws of growth rather than a sudden arrival.

Then there is the occasion when Jesus confessed he had no idea when the *parousia* would happen: 'No man knows the hour, neither the angels in heaven nor the Son, only the Father.'

But he made incidental comments which suggested that it couldn't be imminent. Thus he said, 'You will always have the poor with you, but not me.' Or there are those words spoken at the Last Supper, 'Do this in remembrance of me' – that surely assumed some continuing fellowship of his followers, and therefore the survival of history itself. And why would he choose and train twelve disciples to carry on his work if he thought the world was about to end at any moment, especially since he said that the gospel would be preached to the Gentiles before the End could come?

It was not the timing of the End so much as the certainty and the surprise of it that he emphasized. This element of surprise is the point of the parables of the pearl and the buried treasure; it is not the value of the real estate uncovered but the astounded joy of the finders that is the critical thing. The End will be a surprise to everyone – and a very nasty surprise to some.

It is this element of the unexpected which gives some of the parables of Jesus their tang. Dives, the rich man in hell, is utterly shattered by the unexpectedness of the way things have turned out: those judged to be goats and rejected because they did not feed the hungry and clothe the naked, cry, astounded, 'Lord, when did we see you naked . . . ?'

The End is bound to be full of surprises simply because of God's nature as love, for when any relationship is based on love there is no end to the surprises that may lie in store for those who give and receive it. And the supreme surprise which the God of love could conceivably offer us is the transformation of our present dim sight into the glorious full light of his immediate presence.

What God has in store for us we cannot know, because we have no idea what love might do. We certainly know what evil can do from our own miserable experience. We've been there. But no one knows what love might do.

Yet not everything can be up for grabs, totally unpredictable. There has to be a central core of certainty which allows us the freedom to wander at will wherever the call of love beckons but still gives us a reference point we can get back to when we are hopelessly lost. 'I know in whom I have believed', Paul said again and again to reassure himself as he wandered hither and thither, constantly surprised by what God had in store for him.

There is also something almost ominous in the element of surprise that is at the heart of faith. According to Luke, Jesus says that once the master of the house has locked the door, people may stand outside and cry, 'Sir, Let us in!' and he will reply, 'I don't know where you've come from.' And he then goes on to talk about the first being last and the last being first – a complete overturning of normal expectations and rational predictions.

The *parousia* may surprise us by the strangeness of it, but the truth has been under our nose all the time and we hadn't realized it. We might discover in horror that what we thought was a first-century prophet's rhetoric is sober fact; Jesus does confront us in the person of the outcast, the prisoner, the sick and the naked. Part of the shock of the End will be the realization when we come to judgement that the Judge is familiar to us. He is not a resplendent being from on high but someone who has crossed our path before. Paul tells the people of Athens in the Areopagus, 'God has fixed a day on which he will judge the world in righteousness *by a man* . . .' In so doing he echoes Jesus' words in John's Gospel, 'The Father has given over all judgement to the Son.' So in the catch-phrase of that famous wartime radio show, 'It's that man again!'

Let both grow together until the harvest

Matthew 13.30

It's all very well Christians claiming that this world belongs to God, but the world doesn't seem to be aware of the fact. Certainly, God hasn't had it all his own way in history, which has been a perennial clash between God's purposes and the attempts of evil to frustrate them. Nowhere is this truth put more simply or vividly than in Jesus' parable of the wheat and the weeds. A farmer – and we are given to understand he means God – sows wheat in a field, and during the night an enemy creeps in and plants weeds. The wheat and weeds grow together, inseparable until the harvest, when the wheat is gathered into barns and the weeds are burned.

What Jesus is saying is that history is not the story of inevitable moral progress, as good overcomes evil. On the contrary, the possibilities of evil grow with every advance of good; the more mature the wheat, the stronger and more strangulating the weeds.

The very best actions of which we are capable, twisted by a bent world, let loose a flood of consequences both good and bad. For example, we unlock the energy of the atom: that is good, one more evidence of our God-given dominion over the world; but the consequences of this discovery are mixed. There are creative results such as the cobalt bomb which can destroy cancer cells, and evil ones such as the hydrogen bomb which threatens the future of the human race. But the outward ripples of this discovery do not even stop there. These wicked things – nuclear weapons – have had, paradoxically, the good effect of forcing an uneasy peace on the world because the alternative is unthinkable – in the words of Winston Churchill, 'Peace has become the sturdy child of Terror.'

This is life; not a neat, tidy, morally transparent business, but a murky, ambiguous one through which there is interwoven triumph and tragedy, beauty and terror, majesty and madness, fire and love. The parable teaches us that there is no such thing as automatic progress within history. Change does not inevitably mean improvement, we are not growing daily better and better in the best of all possible worlds.

This interweaving of good and evil in life is so complicated and terrifying that it cannot be unpicked by human effort, however dedicated. There has to be a harvest, a final divine intervention which settles the matter once and for all. Wheat and weeds are not left to rot in the field; it is their destiny to be gathered and separated. This must mean that history will neither drag on nor fizzle out. The conflict between good and evil is not a war without end. There is to be a grand finale when good and evil will be unmistakably seen for what they are and dealt with accordingly.

Fools for Christ's sake
(Shrove Tuesday)

I Corinthians 4.10

In Lancashire, we used to call Shrove Tuesday 'Pancake Day', when traditionally the Church gave its blessing to hearty eating and boisterous behaviour before Christians faced the austerity and fasting of Lent. The fact that Shrove Tuesday is part of the Church's calendar at all demonstrates that far from Christianity being other-worldly, it is very down to earth in its realism about human nature. Knowing the temptation that a larder full of food can pose to believers trying to fast, the Church encouraged believers to empty their shelves of butter, eggs and sugar, turn them into pancakes and eat them on this day so there wouldn't be any forbidden food around to tempt them during the forty days of Lent. If we gorged ourselves every day, it would be gluttony, but once a year it is a celebration of the good things of life. It turned a human weakness into a religious observance and so preserved us from morbid guilt.

It was also a day for putting physical energy to good use. When the pancake bell sounded, people would leave their work in the fields and factories to join in organized fun and games. Even today, there are many towns in Britain where pancake races are run, contestants tossing pancakes from frying pans and catching them again as they dash along the course. Long before fitness and leisure centres were thought of, the Church had recognized that strenuous physical activity can be mood-changing and spiritually beneficial, putting believers into the right attitude for Lent.

Perhaps most important of all, traditionally Shrove Tuesday was the day on which believers were encouraged to make fun of all the important people they treated with great respect throughout the rest of the year. They could poke fun at their rulers, wear grotesque masks caricaturing bishops and tell bawdy jokes about their parish priests. For a few hours they could live out a kind of foretaste of what the kingdom of heaven will be like when everything is turned topsy-turvy, the last become first, the mighty toppled and the poor exalted, when all

34

ranks and titles are abolished and laughter and feasting are the order of the day.

Religious festivals such as the medieval Feast of Fools were occasions when Christians felt able to make fun of all the things, people and rites they took with the utmost seriousness throughout the rest of the year. For a few hours as the holy season of Lent approached, these most pious of religious believers enjoyed a brief holiday from the unremitting pressures of their vocation.

Perhaps the truth is that in times when people were secure in their religion they could afford to be jokey about it. On the other hand, in a secular age swept by doubt and assaulted by a hundred varieties of agnosticism, Christians tend to feel threatened by religious satire. That may be because they have forgotten the Latin root of the word 'religion' – that which binds everything together, the totality of life held by and in God: life and death, time and eternity, spirit and matter, the things which call out tears and those which evoke laughter. You can no more leave out laughter from a religious account of the world than exclude the continent of Asia from an inventory of its land masses.

Shrove Tuesday is so called because believers got themselves shriven; got their sins off their chests so that they could indulge in merry-making with quiet conscience.

LENT AND HOLY WEEK

Because I am Holy, you shall be holy

Leviticus 11.45

The word 'holiness' means to separate sharply, to cut. We describe someone as being a cut above the rest. When we call God holy, we are talking about him being not just a cut *above* everything else but cut off *from* it by an impenetrable barrier of unapproachable majesty.

In the beginning, God's holiness seemed to have no ethical content. It was raw, sometimes savage energy, and to get in its way was fatal, as that poor chap Uzzah in the Old Testament found out when he tried to steady the Ark of the Covenant and was struck dead. Or there were those two priestly sons of Aaron who were burnt to a crisp for indulging in a little unauthorized liturgical revision.

The Hebrew words which describe the inner fire of God's being mean snorting, foaming, boiling under pressure. And when the Old Testament writers sought suitable metaphors for God, they described him as a roaring lion, a hissing serpent, a ravaging beast, and angry bear – untamed power. The poet Walt Whitman wrote that in all true religion there is a touch of animal heat.

So in the human exploration into God, his holiness was encountered first as a sense of dread in the presence of the Holy Other. Then the prophets made one of the great discoveries in the history of religion, for they detected another element in the holiness of God besides transcendent otherness: moral perfection, the sum of purity and goodness and truth and justice. God's holiness was not just energy but moral energy.

They declared God is holy *and yet* a saviour. The classical passage is Isaiah 6. This is probably the most majestic attempt I know to capture the essence of divine holiness in words; one of the most graphic passages in the Bible – a scene of smoke and noise and blinding light; the shaking of foundations, the cry of the seraphim, angels singing, the temple filled with unearthly presence.

Isaiah, understandably, is struck by dread, but something more. He is filled with a sense of unworthiness, moral failure. The human frailty of the most righteous man in the nation is exposed in the presence of God's holiness like a dark shadow on an X-ray plate. Among his contemporaries, in the half-light of human existence, his character shone, but confronted by the holiness of God, his moral being was exposed for what it was. And Isaiah located his sin not as incorrect ceremonial behaviour – failure to give due honour to the Wholly Other – but in his own and his people's unclean living and evil speaking. The holiness of God was not just to be acknowledged in the temple as transcendent Otherness but should be proclaimed in the streets as moral purity.

So the prophets saw God's holiness as a force that makes for righteousness; a crusading power seeking to pour out salvation upon the nations. Isaiah understood his mission as to spread holiness; to claim the nations of the earth for the kingdom of a holy God.

Now this was a great leap forward, but it encompassed a problem. 'God is holy', said the ancients; 'God is holy *and yet* a Saviour', said the prophets. That conditional '*and yet*' involved a paradox. A Saviour God calls us to him; a holy God has no option but to repulse us because of our sinfulness. God cannot just wipe the slate clean and say, 'Forget it!' for it is on his integrity, his self-consistency that the moral order of the universe depends; without it there would be chaos.

The prophets just had to live with these two elements in their understanding of the holiness of God and hold them in creative tension. It was the best they could do until Jesus came upon the scene. He resolved the paradox by adding a final link to the chain of argument – 'God is holy', said the ancients; 'God is holy *and yet* a Saviour', said the prophets; 'God is holy and *therefore* a saviour', said Jesus. Thus the pattern of revelation is complete: holiness is not just raw energy nor even moral energy but redemptive energy.

Jesus revolutionized our understanding of God's holiness by embodying it; all there was of God that could be contained in human form was incarnate in him. Men and women saw, in Paul's word, God's holiness placarded before them, trudging the dusty paths of Palestine, leaving footprints in the sand and blood on a cross, seeking the lost, offering new life and new hope to all he encountered. And the battle-cry of his kingdom was, 'Holy be thy name.' As the pattern of the Lord's Prayer demonstrates, this is the primary confession of the Christian faith; it comes before everything else.

All this renders absurd any notion of God's holiness either as savagery or abstraction. The New Testament images of holiness are boisterous, joyous, noisy. Jesus talked of the lame leaping like deer, the blind seeing, about trees clapping their hands, the tongues of the dumb singing. Holiness is expressed through feasting and festivity in the kingdom of a holy God. In a word, holiness is the happiness of those who are at peace with God through the atoning cross of Jesus Christ.

Christ, the mystery of God

I Corinthians 2.1

The biggest challenge to faith in our day doesn't come from atheists denying God but from believers diminishing him – treating him with cosy familiarity, praying to him as though he were our Old Pal upstairs or singing choruses which portray him as a benevolent simpleton. In this belittling process, God's love is reduced to sentimentality, his power dwindles to benevolence, his wrath becomes regret and his holiness seems like prissiness. In that well-loved hymn, 'God moves in a mysterious way his wonders to perform', William Cowper has the line, 'Behind a frowning providence, he hides a smiling face.' The God we too often project has no frowning providence to hide behind; just the perpetual vacuous smile of a heavenly Cheshire cat.

Our motives are entirely worthy but fundamentally mistaken. God is not the projection to infinity of the nicest person we have ever met. If and when he chooses, he comes to meet us out of dazzling darkness. There is an almost forbidding strangeness about him which renders our cocksure God-talk embarrassingly inapt.

When we are talking about God we are wrestling with ultimate mystery, for this is where all true religion begins – in the awareness that there is a reality in the universe which is not accessible to our senses. We have neither the words nor the images to characterize the essence of divine mystery. 'Mystery' – the Greek term means to close one's mouth, for every attempt to capture its essence in words is doomed to failure.

Part of the problem is that what began as a religious term, 'mystery', has been corrupted in everyday speech. When people talk about a mystery, they are usually referring to an Agatha Christie or Ruth Rendell-type crime story. In fact, crime stories are rarely mysteries; they are actually either puzzles or problems.

A puzzle is a faulty way of looking at something and can be solved by altering one's perspective. The fact that ships did not fall off the edge of the earth was a puzzle to those who believed that the earth was flat, but it was solved when people stopped thinking like flat-earthers. A problem exists because sufficient information is lacking or because that information is not being properly applied. The appropriate use of information solves the problem.

A mystery, however, cannot be solved, it can only be described and explored, and even then inadequately – any light we cast on a mystery only reveals the great mass of darkness beyond it. The mysterious is not just that realm beyond the stars we cannot reach; it is a dimension pervading everything. There's a fascinating verse in the book of Proverbs which states: 'Four things I do not understand; the way of an eagle in the sky, the way of a serpent on a rock, the way of a ship on the sea and the way of a man with a maid.' Now, a sixth-form science student could help out the poor chap who wrote Proverbs – the eagle flies because it displaces air by the lateral movement of its wings. The serpent moves across the rock by the rippling effect of muscles over its ribs. The passage of a ship on the sea is not mystery to anyone familiar with exact navigation; and as for the dealings of a man with a maid, a combination of biology, psychology and any romantic novelist will explain them.

That seems simple enough, but it's not what the author of Proverbs meant. He's not talking about aerodynamics but about the grace and freedom of the eagle in motion – mystery. And the serpent's sinuousness has from ancient times symbolized the power and subtlety of evil – mystery. Nor do the laws of navigation alone determine the ship's destination; there is that mysterious human urge for voyaging, to push beyond all known frontiers. And as for the man and the maid: sooner or later they will find themselves wrestling with the mystery of the other, for the sacrificial and healing power of love cannot be charted by the chromosomes. There is mystery right at the heart of everyday things – and it is here that we encounter the unknown God.

No man can see me face to face and live

Exodus 33.20

Why does God do things the hard way? Why does he clothe himself in mystery? It is a fair question, and I think that the answer is this. If God did not cover himself in mystery we could not share this world with him. We often talk about creation as though its purpose is to reveal God – we've built the whole of natural theology on that proposition. From one angle, certainly, the Bible is the record of God's progressive revelation of himself, but there is another, puzzling theme running through it, of God's apparent hiddenness. Job lamented, 'O that I knew where I might find him!' Even the psalmist who in one mood says confidently, 'You hold my hand', in another cries, 'You hide your face and I am in despair.'

Why might God hide himself rather than reveal himself in his creation? Because if it were otherwise we would be unable to share this world with him. One of creation's purposes is to protect us from the intolerable impact of a reality we could not withstand.

Demosthenes wrote, 'If you cannot bear the candle, how will you face the sun?' And we cannot bear the candle, because we live within the finest of tolerances. If our temperatures rise or fall by a mere handful of degrees, we die. Too much air pressure on us or too little and we implode or explode; too much noise, too much silence and we go mad. We can only bear a tiny fraction of the totality of reality, so how could we withstand the intolerable reality of God? That is why God said to Moses, 'No man can look upon me face to face and live.'

There's a West African creation myth which puts this point rather well. It says that in the beginning God was naked God, sheer God and people were afraid to go near him. So God hid himself in the mantle of creation. He clothed himself in forests in which they could hunt, rivers in which they could fish, soil they could cultivate. And so the story ends: people lost their fear of approaching God and he was as happy as a dog with fleas.

Life within history is only possible because God obscures himself in mystery, for the unequivocal presence of God is his judgement. Once God is unmistakably there, everything is laid bare: past, present, future, our hopes, our dreams, our fears. Nothing is secret any more. Once everything is in the open, the human story must come to a shuddering stop because overwhelming divine presence will paralyse human action. That's why there's mercy in the mystery of God.

For example, suppose I'm an amateur pianist about to give a recital when someone comes along and says, 'Oh, by the way, Alfred Brendel's in the audience.' Now, I'm sure maestro Brendel would be very generous in the way he reacted to my recital even were he privately grinding his teeth to powder. But his magnanimity wouldn't help my plight as I approach that keyboard with fingers transformed into bunches of bananas. Overwhelming presence paralyses action. There is mercy in the mystery of God, for how else could we struggle with and fulfil ourselves in that little bit of reality over which God has given us dominion? How could we ever realize our human potential if we were intimidated by the intolerable weight of divine glory?

I, if I am lifted up, will draw all men to me

John 12.32

There is something about the unknown that attracts us, lures us on. Unless we strive for realities beyond our reach, our spirits shrink. For much of our lives we drift among small things, small anxieties, small pleasures, small talk and small ideas – much of life is taken up with the routine. But it takes the tonic of big things to bring us fully alive.

We rise with excitement and apprehension to the challenge of the unknown. As a climber-poet facing an unconquered mountain put it, 'I felt myself so small, so great.' Especially is this so in the realm of the spirit, for much of faith's value depends on the element of hazard in it.

As Carl Jung said of Christopher Columbus, 'Using subjective assumptions, a false hypothesis and route abandoned by modern navigation, Columbus nevertheless discovered America.' The lure of the unknown was stronger than an endless succession of technical setbacks.

Every year, thousands of people go to Loch Ness hoping to catch a glimpse of the monster, or they wander the slopes of the Himalayas looking for the footprints of the yeti. In medieval times, scholars went here and there, looking for the philosopher's stone that would turn base metal into gold. This is the magnetism of mystery.

Actually, the mysterious element in religion can help us to understand everything else. It is like the sun. We cannot look at it directly and yet by its light we can see everything else. It is both a blaze and a blur; sharply outlining everything while itself remaining as fluid as fire.

So in this way, God's mystery has exercised a kind of fascination for the human mind since time immemorial. Great religious thinkers have ransacked language to find images that would convey this sense of the Holy Other emerging from dazzling darkness. Plato wrote of flickering shadows on the wall of a cave, and there's that beautiful image in Isaiah of God passing by; you can't see him, only hear the rustle of the hem of his garment as he passes: the whisper of God's ways. Paul wrote about baffling reflections in a mirror.

All these images have the same characteristic – they tantalize with the promise that maybe there's a chink of light in the darkness. Perhaps the hem of the curtain may be lifted up so that we can have a glimpse of the reality beyond it.

Coventry Patmore, the Victorian poet, once defined God as a synthesis of infinity and boundary. I suppose the ocean is an everyday example. The ocean is to the ordinary eye an almost limitless expanse of water, but it has a nearer shore, and the waterline shares the same nature as the sea's furthermost deeps, except that it is within reach.

If God is a synthesis of infinity and boundary, who or what stands on the boundary? Who or what shares the mysterious nature of God and yet is within reach? Jesus, said the early Church.

Now the Incarnation does not dispose of the mystery of God; if anything, it deepens it. The author of Revelation referred to Jesus as the Mystery of God. The more we learn of Christ, the more mysterious his nature seems. Many of his sayings were utterly baffling. His family thought him mad and wanted to put him away; his followers continually missed the point of what he was saying. But then, should we expect easy intelligibility on the boundary line between infinite mystery and human existence? If the prologue to John's Gospel is true that in him the Word, the creative essence of God became flesh, invaded a human personality, what would we expect – a simple, straightforward, sharp-suited first-century evangelist? It is one thing to think human thoughts divinely as great saints do; quite another to think divine thoughts humanly as Jesus did. Mystery swirled around him, but it was magnetic. It has continued to draw men and women on, towards Calvary. 'I, if I be lifted up, will draw all men to me.' Not his uplifted voice, but his uplifted cross, the locus of unfathomable mystery had the ultimate drawing power. In some way we cannot pretend to understand, for an instant, one Friday afternoon in a place called Golgotha, what had been shrouded in unfathomable mystery since time began was exposed to the light of day, like a mountain top glimpsed for a moment through thick drifting cloud – the heart of the mysterious God was laid bare.

The goal of the human religious quest, the reason for all the praying and the fasting and sacrifice, the suffering and the martyrdom, was suddenly manifest. Which is why, when every other aspect of Christian doctrine and history is discounted, this lone figure on the cross with outstretched arms has exercised an uncanny attraction to generations. At some level deeper than their minds, they have sensed that in the Place of the Skull the key to the mystery of God was to be found.

We are become fools for Christ's sake (Passion Sunday)

I Corinthians 4.10

One of the oldest images of Christ was painted on a catacomb wall in Roman times. It depicted a crucified figure with the head of an ass. What could it mean? An insult by an enemy, or was it done by the earliest Christians themselves because they realized the essential absurdity of their situation? Here they were, a handful of nobodies, wretched slaves, derelicts, outcasts hiding from the forces of the most powerful empire the world had ever seen. How utterly ridiculous sounded all their brave rhetoric about establishing God's kingly rule over all the earth; how bizarre their claims that a Galilean workman, a crucified criminal, who never travelled more than a few miles from his home village, was the Lord of the Universe. It was a joke.

This image of Jesus as a Fool appears again and again throughout Christian history, in the medieval Festival of Fools, in the antics and teaching of Francis of Assisi. Then in our time, the 1960s, the musical *Godspell* hit the West End portraying Jesus as a Clown, followed by *Jesus Christ Superstar*.

Some traditional Christians were outraged at the flippancy, if not downright blasphemy, of these musicals. This may be because the only clowns they had seen were red-nosed comedians with huge feet who trotted round the circus ring pouring buckets of water on each other, whereas the Fool with a capital F was a subtle character with a deep spirituality that he hid beneath his cap and bells.

For a change of perspective, instead of viewing Jesus as a

tragic hero, see him as a Fool. Indeed, Paul invites us to become fools for Christ's sake. What are the marks of a Fool?

A Fool refuses to accept the limits of the possible. Take Charlie Chaplin, who was a fool of genius in our own age. He does silly things like refusing to accept the laws of gravity. He rides a bicycle with square wheels or walks along a slack tightrope. You don't need a PhD in Physics to predict he is going to nose-dive to the ground. Sure enough he does, but he picks himself up, dusts himself off and tries again. An occasional refusal to conform to the limits of the possible is eccentricity, but he makes a habit of it; it is his style of life.

Jesus had this flair. He was once in such a hurry to join his disciples who were in a boat out fishing that he forgot that it just isn't possible to walk on water. And the universe seemed so stunned by his effrontery that it momentarily suspended the laws of gravity. On another occasion, he showed a sublime disregard for the laws of arithmetic and would not accept the elementary rule that five loaves and two fishes into five thousand mouths will not go. And they did.

Now I'm aware that to take such Gospel miracles at face value, even playfully, has the New Testament scholars up in arms; but I do know that the Gospels record the total impact that an extraordinary personality made on those around him. And at this distance in time, trying to distinguish between what happened and what his disciples thought happened seems futile.

What the Church celebrates as the resurrection is the supreme example of Jesus' refusal to accept the limits of the possible. He would not allow even the ultimate biological law to separate him from his friends. And if you retort, as you are entitled to, that it is insanity to refuse to accept the limits of the possible, I'd have to agree, though I would add that had it not been for those who throughout history have refused to accept the limits of the possible, we would still be living in caves, our minds darkened by fear and superstition, at the mercy of the elements.

The Fool dares to live out his dreams, at whatever personal cost. This Fool, Jesus, set up his kingdom in a tiny backwater of the Roman Empire and declared a handful of peasants to be the pathfinders of a new humanity. He talked and practised absurdities about loving one's enemies, about forgiving and being forgiven as the most sublime human achievements. This colony of clowns dared to live out their dreams, prepared to pay whatever price the world demanded of them. And it is a sober historical fact that these Fools changed the world.

The Fool's working philosophy is that the universe is benign, people are basically good and love will take the chill off the coldest heart. And he's got the bruises to prove it. Some might call him a mug, but it is in fact a kind of deadly innocence that will sometimes melt hearts which iron bars could not bend.

If the decision to choose for love is the act of a Fool, then Jesus was one of the biggest fools in history. He matched love against power, love against authority, love against disease, love against evil. The Gospels describe a classical Fool's progress. People began by laughing with him, then at him, then their laughter turned to mockery, then they began to suspect he was mocking them, so their sneers escalated to hatred and finally they rid themselves of the disturber of their peace.

I suppose this is one explanation for that wall painting of the crucified figure with an ass's head. If someone is so asinine as to live by love in a hard world, he is bound to come to a sticky end. Sure enough, Jesus did come to a sticky end. But with the true Fool's resilience, he bounced back into history. Like quicksilver, he eluded the grasp of those who tried to put him in his place, and when they finally nailed him down, almost before they had turned their backs, his Spirit was bursting out all over the place.

And he was soon at his old game again, wearing down the stubborn human will with his unflagging concern; refusing to accept that human character is immutably fixed at the level of its lowest instincts. He didn't always win. He still doesn't always win. How could he, given the fact of free will? But occasionally the miracle happens – life calls out to life and a withered spirit blossoms, a long-locked door opens, and love entices out into the light someone whom all the coercion in the world could not move.

The last laugh is on Pilate and the power-hungry, Caiaphas and the stern moralists, and most importantly, on death and the grave.

He is gentle and mounted on a beast of burden (Palm Sunday)

Matthew 21.5

Holy Week sees the climax of a power struggle, though one quite unlike any other in history. The comedian Woody Allen says, 'Why doesn't God give me some proof of his existence, like depositing a large sum of money in my name in a Swiss bank account.' That's how most questions about God's power come up. Obviously, we must assume that God's power is operating according to some rules, otherwise the universe would be a shambles. But what are they? Well, the Bible is the record of a long search to discover the rules by which God uses power. And it was Jesus who brought these rules into the full light of day in a number of acted-out parables. And he did so with such authority that afterwards, when his followers were uncertain whether God was responsible for some world-shaking event, they found themselves asking, 'Would the God of Jesus do that?'

Thus, he taught that God is not just power, he is also personality. By addressing God as Father, Jesus cancelled out all notions of God as an almighty dynamo, naked power blasting away beyond the stars. Fatherhood implies a person and a presence, and the totality of divine personality places limits on his use of power. Because he is goodness, he cannot do evil; because he is love, he cannot hate; because he is truth, he cannot lie; because he is wisdom, he cannot do foolish things. God's power is in the sure grip of his personality.

The Gospels offer us a number of parables of God's power at work in and through Jesus. On Palm Sunday, Jesus entered Jerusalem 'gently on a beast of burden' – almighty power in the grip of humility. Then there is that scene in the Upper Room on the day before the Passover where, it is stated, Jesus 'knowing that all power in heaven and on earth had been given to him . . .' did what? Smash the Roman Empire with thunderbolts or confront the Jewish authorities with irrefutable proof he was the Messiah? He took a towel and washed his disciples' feet – almighty power harnessed for menial service.

Here is located the nub of one of the problems of a proud scientific and technological culture. We crave the power God has without being the personality God is. And the result is often catastrophe.

God's use of power is also consistent with his purpose. Power is not an absolute but a relative thing. It is the ability to accomplish purpose. Whether something is powerful or not depends on what you want to do with it. A bulldozer is powerful for tearing up the earth but useless for taking the top off an egg; dynamite is powerful for blasting great rocks but powerless to lull a baby to sleep. What is powerful for one purpose is impotent for another.

This relationship between power and purpose explains the outrage Christianity caused in the Roman Empire. Here was one of the greatest military nations the world has ever known, where power was glory and any evidence of weakness shameful. And along came this group of nondescript Jews preaching a gospel of a broken, dying God reigning from a cross. That was a scandal and an absurdity. How could the cross be described as the power of God?

If your purpose is to dominate, to coerce – power over people – then the Roman machine was power, and the cross spelt impotence. But if your aim is to change human hearts without smashing the human will – power through people – then the cross has proved to be the power of God to salvation.

Whether or not God is omnipotent in general is for the scholars to argue about, but he is omnipotent in this particular: he can do perfectly all that he wills. And what he wills to do is save us. His power is consistent with his purpose.

The highest exercise of power is a willingness to refrain from using it. That's what a parent does when she resists the temptation to overwhelm a child, and exercises patience in order to win willing obedience. It is what God does when he allows us to exist in freedom and responsibility over against him.

It is easy to mistake such divine forbearance for impotence. 'If I were God,' cried Martin Luther, 'and the world treated me the way it treated him, I would kick the wretched thing to pieces!' And so we would. But to go on sending the rain on the just and unjust, allowing the sun to shine on the evil and the good, pouring out divine gifts without reserve on those who ignore the giver? Not us!

Why then does God go on going on? He goes on because his patience is just another word for his grace, which batters down no doors, doesn't take the biggest hall in town or announce its presence with heavenly fireworks. What did Isaiah predict about the way the Messiah would behave? 'He will not strive nor cry aloud, nor make his voice heard in the streets.' Grace operates only by the power of silent appeal.

Wallace Hamilton tells of Colonel Robert Ingersoll, who was a prominent nineteenth-century atheist who used to tour America lecturing on the impossibility of God. He had a neat party trick with which to end his lecture. He would take out his watch, hold it in front of him and say, 'If there is a God, I defy him to strike me dead in the next five minutes.' And as the minutes ticked by, the tension in the hall grew until with, a flourish, he would put his watch back in his pocket and stalk off the stage. But on one occasion the effect was spoilt when a minister called from the audience, 'Does Colonel Ingersoll really imagine that he can exhaust the patience of Almighty God in five minutes?'

The question of God's omnipotence, his almightiness, bristles with philosophical problems, but for those of us who are not scholars, God's almightiness consists in this: he is almighty to save. He who could smash us, stoops to beseech us.

If you are God's own son, come down from the cross (Good Friday)

Matthew 27.41

That shout from a bystander at the crucifixion is not as silly as it sounds. After all, according to reports, Jesus had walked on water, raised Lazarus from the dead and fed thousands with a few morsels of food. Apparently, he could turn nature topsy-turvy, so why not one last clinching miracle, a sort of grand finale in front of the holiday crowds outside Jerusalem, then the Jews would recognize their longed-for Messiah, making the Roman invaders look foolish?

He couldn't come down. Obvious: he was nailed to the cross. But that wasn't what held him there. It was God's inexorable purpose, to demonstrate that love is the most powerful force in the universe and can triumph in any conceivable circumstance, even the ultimate challenge. Calvary was no historical accident, the outcome of a squalid political and religious intrigue; it was the point in time towards which the whole creation moved. Jesus, who was as closely united to God as any truly human being could be, was held to the cross by the adhesive power of God's love for everyone who has ever lived. And such is the mystical arithmetic of his love that, should teeming humanity be miraculously reduced to one unnoticed wretch, say you or me, Jesus would still have stayed on the cross.

We say we'll do our own dying, we'll take our chances and settle our own debts. That's a noble human sentiment. But if we think for a moment of the person or persons most precious to us, are there lengths to which we would not go if love demanded it? Do we expect God to do less for us?

He couldn't come down; and anyway, if he could, he still wouldn't come down. Jesus ended up there of his own free will. 'No one takes my life from me', he said. He was no helpless pawn swept to his doom by the design of evil people and some decent ones as well. This was the incarnation of love, freely entering into the nameless darkness where evil dwells – love put

50

to the test by all the forces that tear human nature and human history apart.

Ponder that interesting detail in Matthew's account of the crucifixion. Jesus was offered wine laced with an opiate, an act of mercy towards a condemned criminal about to die in agony. Jesus refused to drink it. Why? He was no sacrificial beast dragged to the altar kicking and squealing. His was to be a willing sacrifice, made when he was in full possession of his faculties. Under the influence of an opiate he would no longer have an unclouded mind and know what he was doing; it would interfere with his freedom of will. He once said, 'I come to do your will, O God', and that is how he intended to die, willingly choosing that path to the end.

He was not prepared to fail. There are certain limits to human attainment until someone bursts through them – the conquest of Everest, the four-minute mile, walking on the moon. Jesus was the pioneer of our faith who smashed through the barriers that evil had erected to cramp our spirits and distort our humanity. Now he was being put to the ultimate test, and to shrink from it would be to abort the whole enterprise. We would never have known whether he is the prototype of a new humanity pointing to a creation no longer scarred by evil, or merely a holy man, a great teacher, a fiery prophet finally brought low by an alliance of the forces who feared his influence. He would not come down from the cross so that never again need anyone languish in a self-made hell. He provided not a way out but a way through the fundamental human predicament.

But he did come down. The distinctive sign of the Christian faith is not a crucifix, a cross still bearing its human burden, but an empty cross which symbolizes the truth that Jesus is no longer there; he's somewhere else. In fact, he's everywhere else.

Here is true irony. Those who pinned him down to one spot at one time, 'under Pontius Pilate', gave him to the world for all time.

EASTER SEASON
TO PENTECOST

Why should it be thought incredible that God should raise the dead?

Acts 26.8

Let's face head-on Paul's rhetorical question in his speech before Agrippa. There are a number of reasons why people are likely to regard the resurrection of Jesus as incredible. It is incredible because the idea of the dead rising does not tie in with our experience; because there's no incontrovertible evidence for it; because it is now science which defines the limits of the possible and it says the resurrection of the dead is impossible.

And there's another reason for doubt which is domestic to the Church. We live in a time of doctrinal modesty when, in order to match contemporary scepticism, we say, 'People will never swallow that!' Hence, we cast one doctrine after another overboard until what's left to swallow would not keep a gnat alive. The grand doctrines of the faith – Incarnation, Atonement, Resurrection, Consummation – seem much too rich, even for the taste of many modern Christians. It is a revised, simplified, diluted, stripped-down version of Christianity that is now the vogue.

But I would locate the nub of the issue elsewhere. I suppose the obvious answer to Paul's question, 'Do you think it is incredible that God should raise the dead?' depends on what meaning, what force you give to the word 'God'. If it represents a vacuum or a philosophical concept or a vague benevolent power, a heavenly Father Christmas or a Celestial Pal upstairs, then, yes, it is incredible that such a God should raise the dead.

In other words, if we do not acknowledge God as a powerful force in the everyday, the ordinary, why should we expect him to perform the extraordinary? If we cannot find house-room in our minds for the Incarnation, why should we expect the resurrection? This is what Jesus was hinting at when he said, 'If they do not believe Moses and the Prophets, they will not believe even if one should rise from the dead.' If you don't find God in the kitchen or office or home, why expect him to emerge from the Garden of the Tomb?

This is the reason why, according to the Gospel accounts, the risen Christ appeared only to those who were in one sense or another already his followers – not to Pilate or Caiaphas or the casual passer-by on the streets of Jerusalem. He appeared in his resplendent new life only to those who, however fleetingly, got glimpses of the glory shining through his earthly humiliation.

Ah, says the critic, what that means is the resurrection is just wishful thinking, sheer subjectivism on the part of his followers, who desperately wanted the story of their leader to end in triumph rather than tragedy. But to make the vision of the risen Christ conditional on our having faith in him is not the same thing as saying that our faith has created that vision in the first place. To say I can only see a certain distant star through a telescope doesn't mean that the telescope creates the star.

The degree to which it is incredible that God should raise the dead depends upon whether or not we believe he sustains the living. So it is from the logic of everyday life rather than the realms of the supernatural that any arguments should be drawn.

There is the argument from common sense. We have a profound sense of outrage at the wastefulness of a universe that would obliterate in the flicker of an eyelid human beings who are the product of billions of years of evolutionary pain. We rebel against the notion that those whose love and friendship has enriched our lives can vanish as though they had never been. Now, our desperately wanting something to be true does not necessarily make it so. And yet it was Pascal who said that when God wants to carry a point with his children, he plants it deeper than the mind, in the instinct. And every instinct in us says that the meanest, least regarded of those made in God's image, let alone those who have ennobled our lives, are fit for eternity. What did Jesus promise? After claiming 'In my father's house are many mansions', he went on to say, 'If it were not so, I would have told you.' He was assuring the disciples that if their instincts had betrayed or deceived them, he wouldn't let them persist in their wishful thinking.

When we reflect on this world with all its misery, injustice and inequality, its blighted hopes and unfulfilled expectations, the question arises: would *we* have invented a world in which the human spirit is allowed to burn with a fierce bright flame for only a handful of years before flickering and vanishing? There is nothing rational about a world which clings to the lowest, inanimate matter and lets the highest, the human personality, go. If the mountain outlasts the one who conquered it; if Bach's manuscripts are more enduring than the mind which conceived them; if the saint's mummified body is preserved but the soul aflame with God which occupied it is no more; then the universe is a moral outrage and an affront to common sense. If that kind of a world would not satisfy us, why should we assume it will satisfy the God from whom our ideas of truth, rationality and justice emanate?

So, the notion that God might raise us from the dead is slightly less incredible when we bring our common sense to bear on it.

Then there is the argument from the nature of God. Eternal life in the Christian understanding has never been anchored in any faculty or quality of the human personality but in the nature of God as love. And this must confer immortality of some sort, for love is the drive to unite all that is separated in time, space and condition. And it is obvious that in our brief timespan there are many forms of separation we cannot overcome. We shall meet our death as unfinished creatures, but because we have come to know the love of God, the infinite has been joined to the finite, the work of making us whole has begun and must persist until the enterprise is perfected.

Because by faith we have come to share the being of God, the allotted time for the whole enterprise of transforming us has been extended. To put it in spatial language, which is really silly but it's the best we can do, the crux of the matter is that those who have known the love of God last as long as his love lasts. For whatever we make of Jesus, it is fair to say he died to show us that, whoever we are, we matter to God. And since by definition, God must be perfectly consistent, there can never be a time when we cease to matter to him. Therefore we must be the objects of his love eternally. If God loves us, he must love us until the end; not our end but his end, and since God has no end, in the sense of ceasing to be, he must love us eternally.

I don't think the arguments for such a God raising the dead sound all that incredible.

If Christ is not risen, your faith is in vain

I Corinthians 15.17

After the exhilaration of Easter Day it will do us no harm to come down to earth and ponder the uncomfortable truth that the resurrection was not some irresistibly inevitable climax to Jesus' life and ministry. It happened against the odds; and without it, the verdict of history would have been that Jesus was a failed prophet. As John's Gospel puts it, 'He came to his own and his own rejected him.' His life and mission did not generate the momentum to create a new religion. He appealed to his hearers, 'Come to me and I will give you rest', but it was an appeal that went unheard.

There is nothing that happened prior to Calvary which can explain what took place afterwards. There was much talk of a coming kingdom, but it did not appear. No wonder John the Baptist wondered what was going on and sent a message from prison to find out whether the kingdom would ever show itself.

Those precious months the disciples spent with Jesus were doomed to frustration – momentary flashes of understanding being overtaken by deep gloom, utter misunderstanding, impenetrable mystery. There was that brief moment of triumph when the crowd cried 'Hosanna!' as the prophetic King rode into Zion to claim his throne, then it all dissolved into disaster as he fell into the hands of his enemies who had conspired to destroy him.

Nothing in the account of Jesus' brief ministry can account for the passionate Christian belief in the Lord of Life, for the creation of the Church, or for the undertone of astonishment that runs through the apostolic preaching at the revolutionary change in their fortunes. The followers who according to the Gospels blundered around, never quite getting the point, are, by the time of the record in Acts, sublimely confident in their Lord and secure in their faith.

The resurrection is not a sequel or appendix to the Gospel, nor even its climax. It is the reality in whose light the Gospel came to be written.

Of course, one could take away the belief that Christ rose from the dead and much still remains of Christianity – wise teaching, stories of heroic witness, profound testimony to the holiness of God: Jesus would live on as a reforming rabbi, inspired teacher and holy servant of God. But the Saviour has gone; there is no Gospel foundation for any expectation that the whole world is not just redeemable but in the process of being redeemed.

We could live with the knowledge that Jesus was a failed prophet; many of the greatest human beings who have ever lived were despised, rejected and ignored in their lifetimes; only from the perspective of history is their stature truly revealed. But we can't live without Jesus as risen Lord who transforms not just his followers but the whole created order. For only an eternal power could do that. John Masefield wrote a poem called 'The Widow in the Bye Street' which tells of a widow present at the execution of her son. In her prayer for his immortal soul, she refers to eternal life as a way of restoring 'broken things too broke to mend'. Only the new creation for which Christ died and rose again can restore things 'too broke to mend'.

The crunch is this: as it was for the Apostles so it is for every generation of Christians: would our witness be intelligible if Christ had not risen? If so, then our faith may be strong, optimistic, brave, but must in the end be in vain. We would be following a failed prophet; and that is a noble thing to do, but ultimately frustrating, compared to the possibility that we can die and rise again with him and hail him as our victorious Lord.

Who touched me?

Mark 5.30

It is said that more Christians take Communion at Easter than at any other time of the year. And it is fitting that the most popular celebration of the Easter faith should take the form of pieces of bread being blessed, broken and given into our hands, for Christianity from beginning to end is concerned with the concrete and particular – with a specific man, the carpenter's son; in a particular place, Nazareth; at a particular time, 'under Pontius Pilate'. That is what incarnation means. Just as we cannot speak language in general but must speak a particular one, French or German or Hindustani or whatever, so it is not possible to be incarnate in general, in the abstract; we must live and breathe and take up space *somewhere*.

One of the earliest threats Christianity had to fight off came from the Gnostics who offered a flight from the material into an abstract realm of perfection and secret knowledge. They hated the admixture of the holy and the human. They wanted truth without struggle, personality unmarked by evidence of mortality, the spiritual rescued and purified from contamination with the material.

The sacramental and liturgical life of the Christian community was an attack on the Gnostic mind. The Gospel is about flesh being lacerated, blood spilt, about the weight of hands laid upon us, and water taking away our breath as we plunge beneath the healing stream.

The Gospel story is punctuated by material things, loaves and fishes, cruel nails, salty tears, spilt blood, Jordan's water stained by the bodies of countless sinners, an empty tomb. Christianity is a sensual religion, unlike others whose devotees seek to mortify the flesh and fly away to the realms of the spirit. As the author of the first letter of John puts it, the word of life was capable not just of being seen and heard but also touched.

While much higher religion is taken up with esoteric discussions about the being and nature of God, this happens at a level way beyond the poor distraught woman desperate for healing who clutched at the hem of Jesus' robe. There is no room for inverted snobbery in Christianity; we certainly ought not to denigrate those who love God primarily with their minds by exploring complex ideas, but for most of us it is the Word become flesh that counts, something we can get hold of, something reassuringly real like bread in our mouths and wine on our tongues.

John of Damascus writes about the soul's need of visible symbols. 'Perchance, thou art lifted up and set apart from this material world; thou walkest above this body as if borne down by no weight of flesh, and mayest despise whatever thine eyes behold. But I, who am a man and clothed in the body, desire to converse with holy things in the body and see them with mine eyes.'

The general is always easier to cope with than the particular. We find it less painful to pray for the whole vast world and its apparently insoluble problems than for half a dozen people right under our noses where the point of contact between the prayer and the reality to which it refers cannot be avoided. The world in the round cannot make costly demands on us; our neighbour does. It is not the general principle but the particular case that challenges us most. The crowd may swirl around us but it is the one who touches us beseechingly who puts the genuineness of our love to the test. Everything hangs, said Jesus, not on great sweeping theological affirmations but on minute things like the individual hairs of our head, the single sparrow that falls to the ground or the tiny coin lost by a housewife.

In an era of mass communication when many of those who address us do it at a safe distance from the remoteness of the radio and television studio, it is salutary that when Jesus spoke of God's love he was never beyond the range of anyone who cared to tap him on the shoulder and say, 'Prove it!'

One Jesus who was dead,
whom Paul affirmed to be alive

Acts 25.19

It takes some courage to stand up in the vicinity of a graveyard and announce publicly that someone once buried there is alive. In effect, that's what Paul did, much to the puzzlement of the Roman procurator Festus who, when he came to take up office, found Paul in prison and enquired why. He found that there was no evidence to justify Paul's imprisonment. It was the sheer impudence of Paul's claim that Jesus was alive which angered Jews, some of whom had actually seen Christ crucified.

Festus concluded that Paul was mad rather than bad, his brain had obviously overheated from too much study. It was a fair assumption; there is nothing rational about a claim that someone certified dead is up and about, especially if compounded by an insistence that one has actually met him. The most impressive tributes to the truth of Christianity have often been paid by enemies and sceptics. They single out as marks of shame or incredulity those very qualities of faith which are Christianity's enduring glory. And there is often some truth in these allegations. Faith in a risen Lord demands a degree of disregard for natural laws which might justly attract Festus' charge of madness.

Religious scepticism is not a twentieth-century phenomenon. Wherever the Apostles tried to preach the resurrection they found disbelief, for they began to evangelize in the very place where Jesus was crucified and before the very people who had seen him die. What did the early Christians expect other than incredulity, anger and contempt?

Paul himself had cause to be the greatest sceptic of them all. His whole manner of living, the entire structure of his faith, his caste, his race, his profession; all were implicated in the death of Jesus. Between him and the resurrection ran a river of blood, that of Stephen and others he had helped to persecute. Yet Paul insists that Jesus is alive. And if his lips had not declared it, his life would have said it, for Jesus had radically changed him. The love of Jesus had become the greatest reality of his life. During

David Livingstone's last journey across Africa he once spent six weeks in perpetual darkness, hacking his way through dense bush, tropical jungle. Then he and his companions suddenly came out into the light of day. 'Now I know what it means to believe that Christ is the light of the world', he wrote in his *Journal*.

Livingstone had traversed the entire continent of Africa from East to West and back again on foot three times. A tougher, less sentimental Christian there never was, so one is forced to ask: was it empty rhetoric or a pious platitude when he recorded in his diary in a matter-of-fact way, 'I went tramping through Africa in the companionship of Christ'? Or when the seventeenth-century Presbyterian divine Samuel Rutherford, in gaol for high treason, wrote to a friend, 'Jesus came into my cell last night and every stone flashed like a ruby.' Was that an hallucination? Or was it one more evidence of the Apostolic Succession – those who in every generation can claim, 'Christ is alive. We know that because we have met him and live to serve him.' So too Paul: Jesus had brought him out of darkness into glorious light. How could he deny that Jesus was alive?

Our beliefs do not always stand the testing of the years. Faith only exists as a continual inner warfare. The Christ of our glad youth might not offer sufficient certainty for our problematic old age. The certainty of the sunny uplands may evaporate in the valley of the shadow. But the encroaching dark did not force to the surface any religious doubt in Paul. He began his ministry by declaring that Jesus is alive; he ended it with the confession, 'I have kept the faith.' Faith in a living Christ.

They continued steadfastly in prayer ... with Mary, Jesus' mother

Acts 1.14

To no one in the Gospel story does Hamlet's words, 'The rest is silence' more appropriately apply than to Mary, the mother of Jesus. There is only one fleeting glimpse of her after John took her from the place of crucifixion to his home. She is numbered among the Apostles gathered together to pray and ponder over the significance of Jesus' ascension. After the drama of the trial, the agony of the crucifixion, the wonder of the resurrection – great events in which she had a central role as the nearest and dearest of the Christ – there is the apparent anti-climax of sinking back into near oblivion as a mere member of the Christian fellowship.

Mary has always been in the background of the Gospel story, flitting in and out of the life of Jesus, naturally figuring prominently in the accounts of his birth, then reappearing at the foot of the cross and finally in the Upper Room at Jerusalem witnessing the growth of the infant Church. Though the Church was later to accord her great honour and dignity as the Mother of the Redeemer, she plainly sought no central position among the Apostles, even though she must have known more about Jesus than anyone else living. Unlike the reminiscences of those intimate with the lives of modern celebrities and wishing to share their privileged knowledge with the public, Mary did not produce any document entitled, 'My Life with Jesus', or 'Jesus as I knew him'.

To pick up the threads of one's life after great grief; to avoid the paralysis of constantly harping on a traumatic past experience – that takes real spiritual maturity. Mary claimed no special place for herself as one uniquely entitled to mourn a lost son or to bathe in the reflected glory of his victory over death. Instead she transformed volcanic emotion into steady power; tumultuous memories into quiet prayer. She did not hoard selfishly her recollections of Jesus but presumably shared them in the common prayer life of the Apostles.

Harold Lucock quotes the reminiscences of Mrs Thirkell, the granddaughter of the Pre-Raphaelite painter, Edward Burne-Jones. She says that the great artist put one of his most beautiful windows, a representation of the Holy Grail, not in a prominent place in his splendid house but over the sink where the scullery maid washed up. So Mary put her great memories into the common pool of experience where they might inspire the Apostles' ongoing tasks.

Mary's willing acceptance of a modest place among the Apostles signifies her recognition of a changed relationship with the glorified Lord of Life. Even her close human bond was transcended because all the followers of Jesus were able to claim the same kinship with him – a change foreshadowed when in the Gospel Jesus announced, 'Whoever does the will of God is my brother and sister and mother.' It was a new role that Mary accepted without complaint.

In many of our older churches, pictures and images of Mary were smashed because Protestants felt it was dangerous to give Jesus' mother almost equal billing to her Son. Though both Catholic and Orthodox Christians venerate Mary as the Mother of the Redeemer, pre-eminent among the saints, they carefully avoid blurring the distinction in rank between herself and her Son, though some popes have come near to the point by the dogmas they have promulgated. Yet it is precisely when we see Mary the Mother of Jesus venerated with pomp and reverence that we need to keep always in mind as a balancing truth this apostolic picture of the diffident Mary content to remain in the shadow of the more prominent leaders of the early Church. She would probably have echoed John the Baptist's prophetic words about his relationship with Jesus, 'He must increase, but I must decrease.'

Which of you by taking thought can add one cubit to his stature?

Matthew 6.27

The greatest challenge to faith comes not from the blasphemer but from the rationalizer. It is not the enemy who seeks to abolish Christianity who does most damage. History seems to show that the blood of the martyrs is truly the seed of the Church. It is the easy-going friendly rationalizer who wants to make Christianity palatable to a scientifically inclined generation who seriously undermines it by seeking to explain away the mysteries at its heart. For example, he demands the freedom to whittle down the number of Gospel miracles but denies God the liberty to perform more miracles. He will approve of you as a liberal if you believe less than is traditional about the Christian faith but damn you as a fanatic if you believe more.

Like the girl who announced she was only slightly pregnant, he will accept that Christianity has a slightly supernatural element in it. But to profess a full-blooded belief that Christianity is wholly supernatural in the sense that all its power comes from God acting through obedient human beings is dismissed as a mental aberration.

All this rationalizing has its effect on pew dwellers. There was a time when they felt obliged to hide the fact that they knew less about Christian doctrine than their parson; now some of them resort to subterfuge to keep from their parson the horrid truth that they believe more doctrine than he or she does. It is fashionable to dismiss as 'myths' the great central doctrines of the faith without recognizing that human myths may be God's truths. Divinity may choose to inspire Gospel writers with extraordinary visions we moderns dismiss as poetry, literary licence or mythology.

Because Christianity is the historical result of the eternal intersecting and penetrating the natural, it will never be a series of neat logical propositions. It is a sprawling, untidy, even messy story where the limits of language are often reached and loose ends dangle about all over the place. And every attempt through Christian history to tidy up the mess by means of a verbal formula has raised more difficulties than it solved. But the fact that we are dealing with truths which do not fit neatly into words is not an argument for ditching them.

The motives of the rationalizers are honourable but their efforts in offering neat errors in place of untidy truths reduce Christianity to an ideology robbed of fire, poetry and mystery. Far from lending itself to simplification, Christianity is the most complex of all religions. To take just one unique element in it: it adds two attributes to divinity which are missing from other forms of theism – courage and suffering. To create the world was an act of divine courage; to forbear from blotting it out involves divine suffering.

Christianity is finally based on a miracle, a quite non-rational conviction: that a God who can find his way out of a tomb rises to offer new life through a faith which has undergone the full rigour of its death.

History seems to run in cycles. The Christian faith has always had elements which powerfully commend themselves to anyone who cares to explore the meaning of life, and other aspects which seem frankly incredible to them. Once, the miracles of Jesus were the strongest proof of his power and significance; now, they are an embarrassment to many Christians anxious to commend the gospel in a scientifically minded society. Today, it is the divinity of Christ that people find hard to swallow, whereas the early Church had much greater difficulty with his humanity.

So it is with Jesus' death and resurrection. Few people today seriously question that a Jewish prophet called Jesus of Nazareth was put to death for defying religious and secular authority; that is a matter of history. It is his resurrection which many find unbelievable. The opposite was true in the early days. Those who stood nearest to Jesus found it almost impossible to believe that he had really and truly died. They had seen him challenge evil in all its forms and restore wholeness to those blighted by nature, sight to the blind, cleansing to the leprous and health to the fevered. And if the story of Lazarus is to be believed, he challenged death itself and forced it to render up its prisoner.

All this they had seen, and so they could not comprehend that he himself had finally fallen prey to the last enemy. That he should die, that death should conquer him and the grave claim him – that was the mystery they could not fathom. Perhaps this is why, though Jesus warned them on more than one occasion of his impending death, the disciples could not believe it. That he who was the very essence of life should have his life extinguished like a flickering flame was an outrage. But he told his disciples something else which, had they pondered it, might have served to explain the inexplicable. He said that no one could take his life away from him; he would willingly lay it down of his own volition. His death was not a dark necessity but a glorious and crowning act of self-sacrifice as he freely aligned himself with his Father's will.

Once the disciples got that point clear, his resurrection seemed a triumphant inevitability.

They follow the form of religion but will have nothing to do with it as a force

2 Timothy 3.5

There is an inevitable tension between the forms of religion – liturgies and theologies and church organization – and its force as energy, power, spirit. And these aspects of religion do not always march together.

What is the essential force of religion? It is the holiness of God expressed not as some mystical abstraction but as moral energy at white heat. Our God, says Hebrews, is a consuming fire. This is the central theme of the Bible, the holiness of God offered to the whole creation as love and bursting into human life either as grace or as judgement.

So, from the dawn of time we have evolved strategies, rituals, systems, theologies, the forms of religion, for two purposes – to protect us from the full impact of religion's force, and to harness that power, to domesticate God.

Take John Wesley. He ransacked the theological textbooks, the manuals of church order, the sermons of the church fathers – all the sumptuous wealth of Christianity's manifold forms – for clues as to how he, a moral man, burdened with guilt and haunted by the fear of death, might stand in the presence of a holy God. After all, he and his Oxford friends were known as Methodists, people who gloried in the forms of religion, in good order and method. They clung desperately to the form in the hope that it might protect them from the force perceived as divine anger, sinister and doom-laden.

Hiding from the force within the forms: that was the first stage in Wesley's experience. Then came the second: force over-whelming form. It happened at Aldersgate in 1738. Someone was reading from the preface in Luther's commentary on Romans and what struck Wesley like a bolt from the blue was that God accepts us by faith alone, regardless of our spiritual condition or our observance of the forms of religion. Wesley claimed to have heard the words, 'Thou art pardoned, thou hast redemption in his blood.'

Once the force overwhelms the forms of religion – as it does, for example, in revival – it becomes clear that some of the old forms can no longer mediate its force; yet there must be some channels through which the force can flow, so the search is on for new forms.

In the case of the early Methodists, these new forms didn't emerge from the textbooks; they were practical responses to the pressure of the force, as when Wesley handed over the advocacy of the gospel primarily to the laity because he and a tiny band of fellow-minded ministers couldn't be here, there and every-where. Or confronted with a great missionary opportunity in the New World, he risked grievous heresy and ordained minis-ters without episcopal sanction. He evolved the class meeting as a place where converts could share their experience, receive strength from each other in tough times and learn more of the faith. And when the doors of Anglican churches were barred against him, he used the market place, the graveyard or farm cart as a pulpit: new forms to mediate the force.

So this is the sequence: form suffocating force; force over-whelming form and force seeking new forms through which to express itself. But there is one more move in the game. Like the wind, the Holy Spirit comes and goes unpredictably. Martin Luther in a famous passage described the grace of God as a shower of rain that passes over and you must take advantage of it while you can because you do not know when it will pass over again.

The force has a sovereign initiative, and much of the Church's life is spent waiting for it. You might call these our wilderness periods – when we plod on through the desert, seeing nothing but sun and sand and distance, no unearthly visions to inspire us, no supernatural voices to cheer us on. The liturgy puts it well. It calls it proclaiming the Lord's death till he come.

This is the hardest thing any body of believers is required to do – wait. To wait for the signals of transcendence, for an angel to stir the waters of the pool; for the stone to be rolled away from the sepulchre's mouth; for the voice that bids her, as it did Lazarus, to come forth from the grave.

Because we cannot predict when the force of religion will burst into history, into our lives, there are periods when we have to cling to the forms of religion while we wait for its force. We can only go on doggedly proclaiming the Lord's death until he comes. Nowhere in the New Testament is the Church promised worldly success or prosperity. Within history, final victory may be beyond us; our task is to be faithful. There is that pointed question Jesus asked: 'When the Son of Man returns, will he find faith on the earth?' Not, will he find a triumphant Church or a fully realized kingdom, but somewhere in the whole wide world, in season and out, has the Lord's death been proclaimed in word and sacrament? That form is perpetually relevant until it is transcended by the decisive force of Christ's glorious return.

It is expedient for you that I should go away
(Ascension Day)

John 16.7

Christianity as a living faith hangs on two apparently contradictory sayings of Jesus. The first is: 'I go to my Father'; and the
second: 'Lo, I am with you always.' It is what we call the
Ascension that resolves the paradox, holds those statements
together and makes sense of them. For most of the New
Testament writers, with the exception of St Luke, the exaltation
of Jesus is linked to the resurrection rather than seen as a separate
event in the Ascension. Even then it was not a first-century space
odyssey, but a vivid, pictorial way of describing an experience
which transformed the thinking of the disciples over the weeks
following the resurrection.

The disciples went from seeing Jesus somewhere to seeing
him everywhere. I once met a man who was talking about Billy
Graham's evangelical campaign in 1954. He attended a rally
where he had heard and seen Dr Graham on a screen preaching
via a TV link, and he said, 'It wasn't the same as if he had been
with us in the flesh, but he couldn't be in two places at once,
could he?' That's the challenge addressed by the Ascension. How
could an incarnate Christ be in more than one place at a time?
And the risen Christ, though his nature had obviously changed,
was still incarnate: he died and rose again in a particular place;
he met the disciples on the Emmaus road and by the sea-shore.
To be incarnate in one place is to be absent from another.

Just suppose there had been no Ascension. Think of twenty,
thirty years on; imagine posters outside the Church at Corinth
advertising as guest preacher the risen Christ. It wouldn't work,
would it? It is unthinkable that the risen Christ should have
been more intensely present to some believers than others.

Jesus vanished from the disciples' eyes so that he might be
established in their hearts; his physical presence was removed
so that his spiritual presence might remain. For that reason he
said it was expedient he went away. And that process of physical
distancing had already begun when Jesus told Mary in the
garden on the morning of the resurrection, 'Don't touch me!'

She had to come to terms with the strange notion of a form of presence which did not depend on her senses of touch and sight and sound.

When Jesus walked the ways of this earth, leaving footprints in the sand and blood on a cross, only a few, a blessed few, were within range of his voice. Just a handful of his friends in a tiny backwater of the Roman Empire could plead, 'Stay with us, Lord, for it is towards evening'; today millions upon millions of people from earth's wide bounds and ocean's farthest coast can confidently ask, 'Be with us, Lord, in the breaking of this bread; be here and everywhere adored.' Not as a hallowed memory but as a vital presence.

One of the fascinating things about the New Testament is that there is no record in it anywhere of an Apostle or anyone else claiming to *remember* Jesus – that is, treating him as a treasured part of their past. The account of the Ascension in Acts ends with the words, 'They returned to Jerusalem with great joy' – not in tears or sorrowful at the parting of friends, but 'with great joy'. No sense of loss but the beginning of a great new adventure in his company.

The disciples were devout believers, most of whom had been nurtured in that great Jewish tradition which regarded as abhorrent any attempt to capture the likeness of a holy God in picture, word or image. For them, God was the great and unfathomable mystery, the Holy Other beyond the range of their senses and comprehension. Then occurred this great revolution in their thinking as they pondered the significance of the resurrection. Those vivid phrases in the Ascension narrative, 'taken up to heaven in a cloud' and 'seated at the right hand of God' expressed their conviction that Jesus had become an essential part of their idea of God.

After the Ascension it is no longer possible for Christians to see God except through the lens of the personality and life of Jesus; to ascribe any qualities to him which are alien to those demonstrated by Jesus. The Ascension put a face on the unknowable God. To paraphrase Archbishop Michael Ramsey's words, God is Christlike and in him is no un-Christlikeness at all.

And it was expedient for Christ to go away to show that because heaven is his home, so it can be ours too.

I came to cast fire on the earth
(Pentecost)

Luke 12.49

Pentecost can easily become the Festival in the Fog. It lends itself to vagueness and generalized spiritual sentiments. The problem is that, of the three persons of the Trinity, the Holy Spirit is the most difficult to visualize. 'God the Father', that's a strong image; God the Son – well, we have Jesus to feed our imaginations on; but the Holy Spirit – what's there? The very word 'Spirit' suggests formlessness, swirling mist. And the old traditional term, 'Holy Ghost', is even vaguer; you can't strike up much of a relationship with a ghost. The Bible itself isn't always helpful; sometimes it refers to the Holy Spirit as 'He' but in other places, as an 'It'. Now how do you picture a He who could also be an It? Even that ancient symbol of the Spirit, the dove, is a beguiling image, but it suggests beauty rather than power; it is decorative rather than useful.

However, there is another symbol of Pentecost, fire, and there is nothing vague about that. Could there be more definite or forceful statements in the Bible than that reference in the letter to the Hebrews, 'Our God is a consuming fire' or John the Baptist saying, 'I baptize you with water but he will baptize you with fire', or Jesus' own warning, 'I came to cast fire on the earth'? Fire is not to be played around with.

It does one of three things. It destroys. Lorenzo d' Medici was a great showman and impresario in sixteenth-century Florence who laid on huge displays and spectacles, especially at religious festivals. One Whitsun he surpassed himself when he re-enacted the first Pentecost in one of Florence's historic churches. Apparently, with a great roar, tongues of real fire descended onto the heads of the Apostles, but then it got out of control. It burned the clothes off the actors, set ablaze the stage scenery, then spread until the heat cracked the walls of the church and let in a howling gale which fanned the flames, scorching several buildings that stood nearby.

Lorenzo d' Medici's Pentecostal flames consumed the church. There has got to be a moral there. If our prayers were

answered at Whitsun and we were visited by a real descent of
Pentecostal fire, a good many things in the church, some of
which we value, might be destroyed.

One of the things the Spirit burns up is the dead formalism
of church life. Look at what happened to the disciples after the
traumas of the crucifixion and resurrection. For forty days they
were at a loose end, and they did what Christians tend to do
when things drag – they retreated into ecclesiastical bureaucracy, preoccupied themselves with the forms of religion in the
absence of its force. They held elections. They talked strategy.
They battened down the hatches for a rough time as a tiny,
hated offshoot of Judaism.

Then came Pentecost morning which turned their careful
organization into a shambles. The Spirit blasted its way through
their lives like a howling gale, scattering everything in its path.

As with Lorenzo's Pentecost, the Pentecostal flames will
crack asunder the walls we erect in good faith to keep the
gospel safe, contained: they will release it into all the world.
That's what happened at the first Pentecost, the descent of the
Holy Spirit burst out of a sub-sect of Judaism and turned it into
a universal faith. Blown as seeds on the wind, Christianity
spread like wildfire through the ancient world, encountering
alien cultures in places like Rome and Corinth and Athens,
both transforming and being transformed by them into a great
world religion.

What fire does not destroy, it tempers, renders indestruct-
ible. We call Pentecost the birthday of the Church. The Church's
survival is an inexplicable mystery. Jesus told his disciples,
'Upon this rock I will build my church and the gates of hell will
not prevail against it.' Why? First, and most important, it is
capable of springing into fresh life because it has a Lord who
can find his way out of a tomb. But also because throughout its
tempestuous life the Church has been tempered by the fire of
the Spirit which called it into existence and safeguards its
essential identity. We talk about the Church possessing the
Spirit; it is the precise reverse, the Spirit possesses the Church.
The Church does not contain the Spirit as a vessel contains
fuel; the Spirit contains the Church as an ocean contains fish.

Without the Holy Spirit, we would be just one more organization, and a pretty inefficient one at that; our sermons expressions

of opinion; our sacraments hocus-pocus; our authority power-play; our social and political concerns just another form of lobbying; our prayer life formal piety; our ethics conventional morality; our congregations mere audiences; our acts of worship private rituals.

Pentecostal fire has tempered the Church through two thousand years so that Christ's prophecy has been vindicated; the gates of hell have not yet prevailed against it.

Fire welds together. In the face of grim statistics about declining membership and waning influence, many Christians pray at Pentecost for a revival of true evangelical religion, renewed fervour in the Church, a resurgence of powerful preaching, new enthusiasm. That did happen at the first Pente-cost. Hitherto, religion had been a public performance. The ordinary folk stood in the portals of the temple and associated themselves with what the priest was doing at the altar, but they took religion on trust, at second hand. There were a few choice spirits who claimed to have a personal experience of God, and they were known as seers and prophets, rare and exceptional. Then at Pentecost, Simon Peter promised that the Spirit would be poured out on all flesh; everyone could see visions and dream dreams. Anyone had access to the grace and face of God.

So those who expect the descent of the Spirit to increase and deepen personal faith are right. That's what happened. But something else happened too. This collection of individuals who spoke many languages and came from different places were moulded together, welded by the fire of the Spirit into a new community with one heart and one soul, not just for pious purposes but to create a microcosm of a new social order – they abandoned private property, showed fresh care for the poor and a new respect for slaves. Pentecostal fire fused together the personal and social dimensions of religions to turn the faith into a world-changing as well as life-transforming force.

Hear what the Spirit says to the Churches

Revelation 2.7

The Church is primary evidence of the Spirit's working made visible, openly acknowledged. But the Church has no monopoly on that Spirit, which is 'poured out upon all flesh' – not just upon Christians. The Spirit's agenda is more majestic than that of the Church. It is the Spirit in the beginning which broods upon primeval chaos and brings the world into being; it is the Spirit which at the end shows us the holy city Jerusalem coming down out of heaven from God. It is through the Spirit that humanity as a whole is being moulded into the likeness of Christ.

So the first word the Holy Spirit says to the Church is 'Be!' It holds us in being as a people of praise, prayer and prophecy; but supremely of praise. The Church's first task is eucharistic, the offering of praise and thanksgiving – declaring to the world the sheer excellency of him who has called us from darkness into his glorious light. The Church's praise is a thousand variations on a single theme – God was in Christ reconciling the world to himself. Having striven since the dawn of time to find the appropriate tongue in which to address God, at Pentecost the Apostles discovered it in the language of doxology. Our earthly praises are the first stammerings of those whom Charles Wesley described as being destined one day to be lost in wonder, love and praise.

Through the Spirit's command the Church comes into being and is constantly recreated, day by day. It is as though every morning we wait with baited breath for the Spirit's command, 'Be!' We may beg and pray, 'Come, Holy Spirit!' but we must await that imperious summons to gather and confess the Lordship of Christ.

The Holy Spirit's second word is 'Yes'. It affirms and liberates the Church; it calls us to freedom; freedom from sin and death. The Church is not made up of different stuff from the world; it is that part of the world shot through with the redemptive power of God. We are those reborn in the Spirit according to the mercy of God in Jesus Christ. But let's be clear what that means. We are not talking about incorporation into a spiritual ghetto. Rebirth is not intended to produce super-heated pietism; that's not conversion, it is spiritual exhibitionism.

When the Spirit opens our eyes to the overmastering reality of Christ and his transforming power, the change in us is shown not just in our praying and Bible reading and worshipping – we would expect it to affect them – but at the pressure points of our lives. And the pressure points of our lives have to do with our attitudes to power, ambition, sex, money, race, justice. If these are not touched and changed then there has been no rebirth.

To be reborn in the Spirit is not solely a transaction between the individual soul and God, but incorporation into a new creation. Therefore, it works in us both personal regeneration and social transformation. It is men and women justified by God who are liberated to fight for justice in the world; it is men and women reconciled to God who struggle for reconciliation between warring personalities and conflicting groups; it is men and women at peace with God who become the growing points of world peace; it is men and women who exult in the joy of their salvation who add to the gaiety and gallantry of life.

Another word the Spirit says to the Church is 'Know!' It is the Spirit of understanding. A number of times in the New Testament we are told to give a reason for the hope or faith that is in us. And if I were to pinpoint one weakness of our present Christian witness, it would be that because our society doesn't like to be made to think, prefers its ideas pre-packaged like its food, we are in danger of selling short the thoughtful case for Christianity, that philosophy of life based and grounded in the person and teaching of Jesus.

Now, the intellectual case is not the only case for Christianity or even the most important, but there is a thoughtful case for it which is going by default in our day. In our desire to match the scepticism of our age, we have almost become too doctrinally modest to believe in the multiplication table.

Christianity has always claimed to address the Big Questions and it is now only the Big Questions that matter. The Spirit says to the Churches, 'You have got to know in whom you believe and what you believe.'

But the Spirit also says to the Church: 'Wait!' There are two little words in the New Testament which are hard to bear. They are the words, 'Not yet'. The author of the epistle to the Hebrews writes, 'We do *not yet* see all things under subjection to Christ'; Paul cries, 'I have *not yet* reached perfection.' John's Gospel asserts that we are now children of God 'but it is *not yet* apparent what we shall be'.

Not yet. Wait, says the Spirit. And that is the hardest thing for any body of believers to do. We have an almost neurotic hyperactive urge to be dashing about doing good things. At least, that way we feel we're doing the Lord's work. But to wait is very hard. There are wilderness periods in the story of the people of God because the occasions of the Spirit's outpouring are humanly unpredictable. We cannot command them, legislate for them or even foresee them. Jesus talked of God coming like a thief in the night, or of God's Spirit blowing as capriciously as the wind. The Church's times are in God's hands; we can lay the kindling but only his Spirit can provide the spark; we can mould the passive clay but only the Spirit can breathe life into it; we can arrange the skeleton but only the Spirit can command, 'Oh ye dry bones, live!'

These seem to be bleak times for the Church. Some commentators claim that Christians are living in the dead period between the crucifixion and the resurrection that the saints called the Dark Night of the Soul. We must stop our ears to the soothsayers of easy optimism or the prognosticators of doom and listen instead for subterranean thunder – it's a sound much like God smashing his way out of a tomb.

TRINITY SEASON

The Lord thy God, the Lord, is One

Mark 12.29

For many years after Christ's death, converts were baptized into his name alone; the idea of baptism into the Triune Name came much later. In the exciting and confusing early morning of the Church the persons of the Trinity were not at all clearly distinguished because in experience believers couldn't separate the Father, Son and Holy Spirit – at least, not without imagining three Gods. To be a believer in Christ and to feel the presence of the Spirit could not be distinguished. When Jesus promises the Comforter, he adds, '*I* will not leave you desolate, I will come to you.' Paul tells the Christians at Corinth, 'The Spirit of God dwells in you', and then goes on, 'Do you not know that Christ is in you?'

How, then, did this puzzling doctrine emerge? It was hammered out as a way of trying to describe, define and safeguard; indeed, to do full justice to the experience of the people of God. But the experience came first – which is why it is futile to make the attempt to get people to sign up to the doctrine of the Trinity if the reality is foreign to them, especially when so many terms in the traditional creeds such as 'person' have changed their meaning. The New Testament confronts us with three dominant symbols of God which we can and should use to express our awareness of God, though there is an area of creative overlapping in them. But if we go beyond this and try to evolve a firm formula, we must recognize that it can only serve, as the hymn says, to be 'our guide and not our chain'.

The Father is the author of all that is, the self-sufficient being on whom all else depends; the Son or Word is the agency by which the hidden God emerges and makes himself known, supremely for our salvation – and the Spirit flows from the

Father through the Son to creation, entering so intimately into our lives that we might claim that God dwells in us. Or we could say that the Trinity summarizes the gospel for it tells us who God is, the Father; what he has done for us, the Son; and what he still does through his indwelling Spirit.

At the Creation, God declares it is not good for a man to live alone. Perhaps it's not good for God to dwell alone either, so he is revealed as a social being.

C. S. Lewis offered what has become the most popular way of visualizing the Trinity. Some theologians have been very sniffy about it, but if it helps, this is all that matters.

Imagine, he said, an ordinary Christian kneeling down to say his prayers. He is trying to get in touch with God, but he knows that what is prompting him to pray is also God. God inside him. Again, he is aware that his most reliable knowledge of God has come to him through Christ, who is standing beside him, helping him to pray. God is the one he is praying to, God is the one inside him pushing him towards his goal and God is also the road or bridge along which he will travel towards that goal. This is how the early Christians experienced God, and when they worked it all out, the best they could do by way of explanation became the doctrine of the Trinity.

The theologian and Anglican monk, Harry Williams, sees it another way and explains how the Trinity copes with two threats to which every person is subject; and since God is personal, he too must face them. One is isolation. From our childhood we fear being left alone, we need relationships for our fulfilment. But we also fear the opposite danger – absorption, losing our identity. In the Trinity the threat of being isolated is overcome because the one God is eternally in relationship; nor is there any danger of the pendulum swinging in the direction of absorption because the three persons of the Trinity are eternally distinct and unconfused.

Just as the Messiah was a concept that first-century Jews felt at home with, so the Trinity was in line with fourth-century Greek thought, though the three-persons-in-one concept is hard to reconcile with modern scientific knowledge of what personality entails. Nowhere is the Trinity spelt out in holy Scripture, though there are a couple of passages, in Matthew and 2 Corinthians, where the Christian 'Grace' is offered.

When dealing with the God who is Wholly Other and beyond the range of our senses, we have no option but to think in terms of models and analogies which are crude representations of ineffable truth. It was the best the early Church could do as an explanation of how God had dealt with them. It was a majestic achievement which has fed the devotional life of Christians ever since.

A man sent from God whose name was John

John 1.16

The ministry belongs to the whole Church; indeed, the whole Church exercises a ministry in which there is no discrimination in spiritual status between the ordained ministry and the laity. But Trinitytide is traditionally the time when the call to the ordained ministry is emphasized, and in some churches ordinations take place on Trinity Sunday. So it is fitting that we should celebrate those called to the full-time service of the Church in its ordained ministry.

This verse is the first reference in that majestic theological account of creation in the prologue of John's Gospel to any human agency being employed. A man sent from God. Or she could be a woman. Let's settle for this: the parson is a human being – a statement the average congregation will receive with the hoots of derision reserved for a fool who told them he had discovered that two and two makes four. Yet good Christians who are well aware that two and two equals four still behave as though a parson were not so much a human being as a disembodied bundle of virtue they pay to be good on their behalf.

Why God chose human beings to be his messengers is his mystery. It must have something to do with the nature of Christian truth which doesn't exist in a vacuum but is incarnate in human personality and gains special authenticity from being wrung out of our doubts and uncertainties. Maybe redeeming truth becomes incarnate in people like us to point the moral that if we can make it our own, then anyone can; if the gospel can transform us, there is hope for everybody.

The world finds it hard to accept that ministry can be truly exercised through full-blooded personality. During the Second World War, a notice was displayed in Employment Exchanges which ran: 'All persons in the following age groups are required to register for National Service except lunatics, the blind and ministers of religion.' Apparently, they thought the minister a special case, exempted by heredity or providence from the more full-blooded of human characteristics, unavailable for worldly service.

Human personality is all about individuality. That is the unique gift anyone brings to the ministry. One of the old rabbis said that God never does the same thing twice. Name any of the great ministerial heroes of the faith: never again will their like be seen in the Church. That precise combination of strengths and weaknesses any human being displays cannot be replicated. The minister is a human being with all that that means, so he or she must not subjugate their individuality because they believe they'd be better ministers if they were a replica of one of their heroes or ideals. God doesn't work through carbon copies; only originals.

Implicit in the notion of being sent is the recognition that someone comes from the outside. In one sense, the parson is always an alien, coming into a situation from the outside and then sooner or later tearing up roots and moving on elsewhere. It can be painful for a congregation to adjust to an unfamiliar figure in the pulpit, a strange family, an unfamiliar way of doing things. It can also be stressful for the parson's family as well. But the semi-nomadic life of the parson proclaims the central biblical truth that our salvation always comes to us from outside. This parsonic wanderer on the face of the earth is a concrete reminder to the people of God that there may be many things they can do for themselves, but they cannot save themselves.

The idea of being sent from God also speaks of the minister's call. There are a few choice spirits who seem to bear out Jeremiah's sense of call, where God says to him, 'Before you came out of the womb I consecrated you and made you a prophet' – those who from childhood have never doubted they would end up in the ranks of the ministry; Archbishop William Temple at the age of five would stand on a stool and preach to the assembled household; there are some parsons whose sense of conviction that they are intended for the ministry is borne in upon them as though someone had tapped them on the shoulder or spoken into their ear: a conviction which has never wavered or diminished.

But there are others whose road has been a winding one, whose motives have been so mixed that only on looking back do they realize that their call to the ministry was a genuine one. They are where God intends them to be – but what a close call it was!

At the heart of this great theological statement about God's creative word carving all things out of nothingness, we stumble across this oddly human touch – a man's name, John. Obviously, if there is a point at which the whole operation is going to break down it is just there, for John or Jane are not ciphers for irresistible power but frail human beings, vulnerable and dependent, creatures of flesh and blood with a breaking point; and they will often reach it.

It is an amazing act of faith that God places his ministers in the hands of the laity. Just as God in Jesus put himself willingly at the mercy of humankind, the minister is at the mercy of his or her people. He is dependent not just for the sinews of life but also for forbearance and support. Who ministers to the minister? I suppose according to the tradition, the Bishop or circuit superintendent. But at another level, in the intimate daily commerce of life it is the people in the pews who have the power to make a minister's life a radiant testimony to the gospel or a living hell.

Perhaps, in the end, a congregation gets the minister or priest it deserves, and this, not because the selection procedure is infallible but because sensitive and caring lay folk can reinforce ministers where they are weakest and multiply their strengths. Modestly gifted ministers have exercised a powerful influence because their people sustained them; ministers of towering ability have come crashing because the insensitivity or hostility of their people were like leaden weights on their feet. Indeed, so pervasive is this mutuality between minister and people that when, tragically, a parson must be accounted a failure, the people would be wise to ask not just 'Where did he or she go wrong?' but 'Where did *we* go wrong?'

Just as God's powerlessness embodies his judgement, so the minister's powerlessness confronts the people with a kind of judgement. When a child is given a name at baptism, that name, John or Jane, symbolizes a solemn obligation on the Church's part to cherish, support and strengthen them. The minister too has a name, and a soul to be saved.

And Moses took the serpent by the tail and it became a rod as a sign

Exodus 4.4

This is one of the most evocative images in the Bible, of wild power being tamed, of the fiercely independent spirit taken in hand and made useful – the serpent become a rod. It graphically illustrates the strange, fascinating, miraculous process which makes a man or a woman a minister and it offers this picture of the ministry as a rod in the hands of God.

It is not a bundle of straw or a lifeless piece of wood that becomes a rod in God's hands but a wriggling serpent – and the serpent has always been symbolic of human passions and instincts that hiss and coil and are always in danger of getting out of control. Sixteen years in central Africa taught me a lot about snakes – I know that no two are identical in the colour or conformation of their scales. They are not just wild but individual, just like priests and ministers; and ordination is not the spiritual equivalent of that hot wire drawn across the brain of disturbed people to subdue them. I remember with gratitude and celebrate the rich diversity of human types God puts to work for him in the ministry. The serpents become rods in his hand – the rumbustious, the reserved, the debonair, the conventional. Under their uniform exterior there is a riot of idiosyncrasies.

Throughout the Bible the rod is a symbol of authority – from Moses raising his rod to heaven and calling down thunder and lightning on the Egyptians to the rider on the white horse in the book of Revelation with the legend 'Word of God' inscribed on his thigh who in an apocalyptic vision is to rule the nations with a rod of iron.

Understandably, Protestants treasure the doctrine of the priesthood of all believers, so they are always tempted to play down the notion of ministerial authority. But the New Testament itself will not allow us to make any concessions to that prevalent disease of our day, pseudo-democracy gone mad. The author of Hebrews writes, 'Remember those who bear rule in the Church because they speak the word of God'; Paul asks the Thessalonians to esteem ministers highly in love for their work's sake.

So the minister rules in the Church, though the essence of that rule as Christ demonstrated is utterly self-denying service. If the minister speaks from an elevated position it is a cross; if he or she wears a crown it is composed of thorns; and the seals of office are a towel and basin for feet-washing.

The serpent become a rod also speaks of the minister's sacramental significance. If some parts of the Church are given to projecting a view of ordination as a mystery sacred to the point of incomprehensibility, nonconformists are prone to the contrary vice, of de-sacralizing ordination to the point of invisibility. What is the sign or sacrament of Christ's one essential ministry in the Church? The ordained ministry is Christ's sacramental gift to the Church, just as the Church is Christ's sacramental gift to the world. That, surely, is the burden and glory of the ministry of Word and sacrament – the minister is more sacramental than the elements he or she handles, just as man is more than the sabbath and Christ than the temple. Is not the supreme sacrament holy personality – taken, blessed, broken and given for the life of the world? The minister's sacramental power lies in offering himself or herself as the means by which not material elements but human lives can be changed. And just as bread and wine are nothing much, but through the power of Christ present at his table become supremely significant, so the ministry is in itself nothing much, but in the hands of Christ assumes a significance not of our deserving but of his choosing.

Sacraments symbolize grace made visible, so the ordained ministry is the Church made visible, though as with an iceberg so with the Church: it is not the most obvious fraction which is the most important. The ordained ministry is the Church made visible in two senses. First, in symbolizing the form Christ has given it. The ordained ministry is a sign that the

Church has a constitution and structure. It is not an amorphous heap like a swarm of bees nor a swirling pink mist of religiosity; it has a shape and form like a body. A body that can be identified, which can be crucified and glorified.

God tells Moses that the serpent has become a rod as a sign. The verse goes on, 'so that men will believe that the Eternal, the God of Abraham, Isaac and Jacob has appeared to you'. That's the nub of the matter. Hebrews says of Moses, 'He endured as seeing him that is invisible.' The minister or priest insists on trying to see what is not visible to unbelievers. This explains why the ministry will never be totally intelligible in a secular world.

THE LOVE OF GOD

God is love

I John 4.8

No word in the English language is more elusive than 'love'. And when we talk about God's love, its resonances with our own experience bring it so easily into the context of earthly relationships that God's radical Otherness is compromised. So much so, that though the phrase 'God is love' is of course scriptural, it is probably wise to add a qualifier such as 'eternal' or 'redeeming' or 'gracious' love.

Even so, we are adrift on a limitless ocean. Paul in Ephesians 3 memorably sketched out the majestic dimensions of God's love. All existence has its being within them – history within its length, creation within its breadth, heaven in its height and hell in its depth. It encompasses everything – the world, life and death, all things present and to come. There are no moral voids, no profane spaces in the universe. Even when our sin separates us from God, the gulf is filled with his love. As the hymn puts it, even the silence of eternity is 'interpreted by love'.

Nor is it possible to consider any aspect of the Christian faith, to discuss any Christian doctrine without finding behind and beyond the particular theme the universal reality of love. What is faith but divine love recognized; hope but divine love's triumph foreshadowed; revelation but divine love doing a new thing; conversion but divine love given best; salvation but divine love at peace? And on and on. 'God is love' is the subtext of all sermons.

The scientists talk of a Theory of Everything; Einstein spent his final years trying to evolve it – a mathematical formula summarizing all we can know about measurable reality, a few symbols that sum up physical life in the universe. Christianity too has its Theory of Everything expressed in the simple formula, God is love.

And it is not only to the sphere of personal faith and devotion that this doctrine is relevant. It has insights to offer to the hectic world of politics and international affairs. One journalist said sardonically, 'All the Church has to say about the state of the world can be summed up in that bald cliché, "God is love."' Clichés may be banal but they tend to be true. Love gives us the power of imagination to put ourselves in someone else's shoes and see how our actions and words look from the other side of the tracks, south of the equator or on the wrong side of the breadline.

What the bald cliché teaches is that in the end our engagement is with God rather than with an economic crisis or political dilemma. The root of many of society's most clamant problems does not lie in the technical aspects of international affairs but in the lack of trust and mutual respect among its members.

All in all, it is hard to bring this unutterable truth about God being love within the range of our minds and imaginations without it being degraded or distorted. Martin Luther once claimed that he could derive the whole of Christian theology from the one word 'thy' in 'Thou shalt love the Lord thy God.' We could do the same for divine love by bringing it to a burning focus in one word – 'Father'. Jesus said, 'Father'. Again and again he said it. It is the last, the final word in the personification of divine love; indeed, in the naming of God. You can't get beyond it, behind it, narrow it down further, transform it into a more accessible metaphor, popularize it. That's it. It is the terminus in human understanding of God.

And by tracing the way humanity has responded to that one word 'Father' in the Bible we can share in its dawning understanding of God's love. I am not suggesting we can detect any hint of change or development or evolution in God's nature as we move through the Bible; it is our human perceptions of him that are at issue.

Like as a father pities his children

Psalm 103.13

I suppose the general thrust of humanity's growing understanding of divinity is the move from God as Maker to God as King – from a deity responsible for our bare origination to one who governs us and controls our lives for appointed ends.

But because of the Covenant, the people of Israel never went along that route. 'I am the Lord thy God who brought thee out of the land of Egypt' – that was the triumphant assertion which rang in their ears from time immemorial. In defiance of the accepted logic of religion, it's as though the Jews heard not just a gospel within the law but a gospel before the law. They knew God as a deliverer before they knew him either as Creator or King.

The Jews cared nothing for theology generally, for all the problems of belief in *a* God; it was *the* God of our fathers, *our* God, *my* God that preoccupied them. They didn't say: here is the general principle of divinity and it works out thus and thus in our life and experience. They moved from the specific to the general – from *our* God backwards to the notion of God as creator and outwards to God as sovereign.

There is no higher understanding of God's love in the Old Testament than the prophets' proclamation of him as righteous king and saviour of the nation. But their consciousness of his holiness constituted a barrier they could not overleap in order to rise beyond divine sovereignty to Fatherhood. True, they used the term 'Father' but only to describe God's relationship to the nation. With one possible exception, they never talk of him as the Father of individual believers.

So it seems as if the psalmist's assertion about the fatherliness of God – 'Like as a father pities his children' – is a personal inspiration rather than a general advance in religious revelation; one of those gleams of vision in which Israel transcended its own genius. It is not that 'Father' as a divine name was a taboo word. The underlying idea just hadn't dawned.

It is not to disparage the psalmist's insight to say that 'like as a father' is an image he imported into God by analogy from human experience. It is our frailty, weakness, suffering, mortality which apparently God pities. And it is precisely in this understanding of God's love that many people in our day rest. They are a good proportion of that 70 per cent of the population who surprisingly year in and year out tell the opinion pollsters that they still believe in God. They are on this side of the great divide between cosmic purpose and meaningless chaos. They do believe in a fatherly God who is a sort of healthy essence, a benevolent fate generally well disposed towards us – a providence of sorts, making personal piety worthwhile and the yearning for God's rule a splendid ideal.

And all this is a long way beyond blank atheism. The bare recognition that God is compassionate love is a giant step forward in humanity's religious quest, and it cancels out notions of him as a dark and fearful force on the one hand or as a cold and abstract proposition on the other. But the problem is that any belief in God solely as compassionate love is challenged by a thousand and one everyday experiences, ranging from natural catastrophe to human wickedness. When that famous earthquake in eighteenth-century Lisbon demolished most of the city, what also perished in the rubble, as Wesley pointed out in his famous pamphlet, was Enlightenment optimism, the notion of a beneficent God, a fatherly, compassionate deity who provides for the well-being of all creatures.

This beneficent deity dies in every generation; dies again and again as the bombs explode, the seas smash the barriers, the buildings crash, the starving children fall before our eyes. It takes a very mature understanding of God's love to believe that the world in its tragedy and grandeur is unfolding as one great divine creative act – as when Paul makes the truly astonishing claim that all things work together for good for them that love God. All things. However calamitous in its immediate consequences, whatever comes our way is blessed in its ultimate effect. That's what Paul meant by the victory that overcomes the world. But it's not what popular piety wants to hear.

And when earnest calls upon God's compassionate love do not produce a miracle in particular cases, when good deeds go unrewarded and evil deeds unpunished, then popular piety flickers and dies. And when we ourselves commit grievous sin, a fatherly God who tut-tuts at our plight won't do. The defect is not in God's compassion but in our imperfect understanding of it. But that's an easy thing for us to say on this side of the Incarnation. Compassionate love is infinitely better than nothing, but it is not enough.

I will arise and go to my father

Luke 15.18

What is faith but the response of a child to the Father's call? How better might one characterize the Christian life than as a going to the Father? There is a direction, a discipline, a terminus in it. We need not charge around in all directions like headless chickens nor be pushed about by the dumb forces of fate. We are on a journey, and whither are we bound? We are going home – not into the unknown nor to dust but to our Father's house.

The basic condition of fallen humanity is homesickness, alienation from God, our neighbour and ourselves. This is the human saga. We are all somewhere along the path between the far country and home, a journey inspired by crisis, undertaken in faith, beset by danger, and we hope accomplished safely in due time. Some may travel quickly and well; others have a hard, perilous time with many detours.

And the parable of the prodigal son has this strong grip on our imagination precisely because it assures us that in spite of our failure and sinfulness there is a warm welcome awaiting us when we reach the father. We know that this is so because the father described in the parable represents all that is best in paternity as the human race has known it – patient, good, wise and infinitely kind.

And yet . . . we must be careful not to be led astray by reading into the parable of the prodigal the totality of God's nature. Like all parables, the story of the prodigal son was not intended to expound a complete theology but to light up a single point, the liberality of God's grace. Indeed, there is no character who fulfils the Christ-role in the parable at all. And it could be argued that a dramatist looking at the story would probably conclude that in terms of its inner dynamic, the chief protagonist is the elder son.

And note that the parable itself carefully avoids any simple identification between the hospitable father and God. At one point, the prodigal confesses, 'I have sinned against heaven and before thee . . .' *Against* heaven, that is, God, and in the presence of a sorrowing witness, the earthly father. So Jesus could not have intended to convey the idea that the father in the parable is God.

Yet God is the injured party, for though you can ill-use your earthly father you can only sin against one who is holy. Only one is Holy – and he is not the father in the parable.

The parable is a beautiful evocation of one aspect of divine love which draws on human paternity at its best. But there are two problems with it as an adequate account of God's love. Whether divine Fatherhood evokes wholesome sentiments depends very much on the individual's experience of human paternity. It is said that Martin Luther, who hated and feared his human father, could not bring himself to describe God as 'Father' without a shudder. As the old preacher said, the child who does not find something of God in his father is unlikely to find a Father in God.

And the other problem is that once back in the Father's house we tend to forget the experiences of the far country. True, we still feel gratitude and gladness. We painlessly merge again into the household of faith, a genial, refined spiritual existence devoid of blood and sweat and wrestling and pain. We find ourselves within the enervating cycle of constant contrition and forgiveness.

If misreading God's compassionate love encourages a chirpy piety which shatters like glass on the unyielding rocks of human experience, so misunderstanding his forgiving love can easily foster effete discipleship – the kind of religion once castigated by Richard Niebuhr as belief in a God without wrath who brings people without sin into a kingdom without judgement through a Christ without a cross.

There is more to the cost of fatherhood than Jesus put in the parable. None of Jesus' parables could carry the whole gospel because they were spoken by one whose main work was still ahead of him.

For much of his ministry Christ talked only of forgiving love. Only at the end did he speak of his blood, pointing to a darker, grimmer, more mysterious fate that was to befall him. Our best understanding of God's forgiving love is both a beautiful and a more rigorous thing than we will often allow, but it is not enough. Think of John Wesley's two lesser-known conversions before Aldersgate in 1738. In 1725 his reading of Thomas à Kempis and Jeremy Taylor transformed the lightheartedness of his college days into a new seriousness towards God. Then two years later he had that spontaneous illumination of God's surpassing glory, when he was persuaded that he was in a state of salvation. On those occasions he surely asked for and received the forgiveness of God. Why then was Aldersgate necessary in 1738?

That thought moves us on from God's forgiving love to his redemptive love.

Jesus said, 'Holy Father'

John 17.11

We noted earlier the majestic dimensions of God's love as sketched out by Paul. But there is something even higher than the height of God's love and lower than its depths – if you like, it is his God-ness, his inner essence as divinity, his holiness. 'God is love' is a sublime truth, but it is not the whole gospel in a nutshell. God is *holy* love, *that* is the whole gospel in a nutshell. God is not just our loving Father, he is our holy Father, and the distinction in action between the two dramatizes the difference between forgiveness and redemption.

A father who is patient and infinitely wise can freely forgive at the cost of grief and wounded affection. It is an individual matter. But, to use the old language, a soul cannot be saved in isolation from a whole world; to redeem us, our sin must be destroyed and that meant not a minor action on God's part but the reorganizing of the universe. We have not just erred and strayed like lost sheep; we have embraced mutiny; the crew have taken over the ship. The challenge is not simply to restore the prodigal son to his home but to transform the moral condition of the entire household.

The one thing a holy Father cannot do for us without reducing the universe to moral chaos is to wipe the slate clean as a merely loving father might do and say, 'Let's forget it.' His holiness demands that he either inflict – why baulk at the word? – penalty or assume it. That's what he did, upholding the law of his being as holiness while saving us to the uttermost.

I don't pretend to understand the nature of the cosmic transaction which took place on the cross, for it happened within the being of God himself and is an awesome mystery, which is why throughout its entire history the Christian Church has never officially adopted any single theory of the Atonement. P. T. Forsyth said that in the death of Jesus, God was present, therefore Jesus experienced the cost of sin as only God can do – for only God can absorb the totality of human sinfulness – but he experienced the effects of sin as only a man can do, for unlike God he could die.

'In the atoning cross of Christ the world is redeemed by a holy God once and for all. There, and only there, sin is judged and broken; there and only there, humanity is reconciled and has access to the face and grace of God; there, and only there, a new creation unscarred by mortality and sin comes to birth.'

We are now at the crux of the whole matter of God's judgement. The critical question, as John Wesley discovered, is: how shall we be able to stand in the last day before God when his love draws us to him but his holiness must repulse us because of our sin? There is only one standing ground. To use classical evangelical language: we must be brought to the foot of the cross.

The God who spared not his own Son will not scruple to bend the most dreadful eventualities to his purposes. He makes the forces that rage against him work to accomplish his ends. To redeem the world cost God's love more than to create it, for the new creation, unlike the first, is not fashioned out of nothingness but out of wreck.

So, once we are within the sphere of God's redeeming love, sin may still be a lapse or an episode but it need no longer be the driving principle of our life. Sin flares in us but it no longer reigns in us. The redemptive love of God has freed us for ever.

This is why judgement begins at the Church. We know who he is and what he has done for us; we know that we can be free. If we put ourselves under thrall again there is no excuse.

———————

The Father has given over judgement to the Son

John 5.22

God respects the integrity of the human personality, and since love requires that both parties must be free to be themselves, therefore there has to be the possibility that the last human word uttered in the universe might be 'No'. And it is this awful prospect which puts the drama of the Last Judgement in its true perspective and silences any sentimental claptrap about the love of God.

Put starkly, if we do not receive God's love as redemption we apprehend it as wrath. But we must be clear about what we are saying. Just as we must not reduce God's redemptive love to purely human emotions in human fatherhood, so we must not distort his wrathful love on the analogy of purely human impulses of anger. St Augustine wrote that God's wrath does not disturb the tranquillity of his mind. There is no heat, fire or aggression in it. And the Lord turned and looked on Peter, and Peter knew. No condemnation, no fury. A sorrowful gaze apprehended as a wrathful one.

The wrathful love of God is not insensate fury but implacable purpose. God has no more anger against us when we flaunt his will than a brick wall we crash into is showing its displeasure by flattening us. This is why Paul reserves the concept of God's wrath not for an attitude of God towards us but as the inevitable consequence of cause and effect in a moral universe. The arithmetic must add up in the end. All accounts must be settled because, if anything has been overlooked, has been forgotten, it cannot be redeemed.

When George Bernard Shaw was asked by a young man for good advice on living he said, 'Find out which way the universe is going and go with it.' 'Come, inherit the Kingdom prepared for you from the foundation of the world' says the great King in the parable. That's the way the universe is going. We are structured for the kingdom as the eye is for light or the heart for love. We are born to believe. We don't wake up and say in disgust, 'I behaved like a Christian last night! I feel terrible!' As Tertullian said, 'The soul is naturally Christian.' That, as the computer experts would say, is our default condition, our built-in bias, and to try to live any other way is to move against the grain of the universe, which means fighting one's way in the teeth of God's love.

According to one of the Gospel stories, God is the quintessential Quaker: he accepts our Yea as Yea and our No as No – that's what love as ultimate respect for the other's right to be themselves must mean. Which takes us back to that parable we have already considered, the healing of the ten lepers. Jesus heals all ten; but only one, a Samaritan, returns to thank him. The other nine go their way and resume their old life, and Jesus accepts their decision without protest or complaint.

The moral, again, presumably is that God in his own ways and times makes himself known to us. And if we are unmoved by him, the danger is not that in his anger he may consume us but that he may accept his failure with us without protest. That is God's love as wrath – his grave and calm acceptance of our autonomy.

Humanly speaking, that is an appalling prospect, or it would be were it not that the Father has given judgement over to the Son. And because we must not compartmentalize God's love, if the cross demonstrates the highest expression of God's love as redemption, then it must also be its clearest outworking as wrath – 'whilst we were yet sinners Christ died for us . . .' and if we continue to sin, what does he do then?

We have no biblical evidence to assume that in another life there will be an even more complete expression of God's love than the cross reveals; or that God will use some unimaginable supernatural power in some unimaginable supernatural realm to turn us to him. The cross is not the last demonstration of divine mercy before the final abandonment of the sinner; it is the supreme assurance that God's love is never exhausted.

According to an image in the book of Revelation there is a

bleeding lamb rather than a resplendent King on the throne of the universe; God in his sacrificial rather than judicial aspect is supreme. This must mean that there was a cross in the heart of God before there was one on Calvary, and ever since. When, then, will it no longer be possible to turn and cling to the old rugged cross?

'Lord, show us the Father and it is enough', says Philip. Jesus replies, 'He that hath seen me hath seen the Father.' The great equation of God's love is resolved, the majestic circle whose sweep encompasses all reality is complete.

'Where art thou?' was the first question God addressed to Adam and Eve at the dawn of the world. And if human love cannot bear separation, how much less divine love; therefore I dare to believe that 'Where art thou?' is the final, anxious question which will ring throughout the new creation as the Father whose nature is holy love strives to ensure that none is lost. Wrathful love indeed.

PROPHETIC RELIGION

Would that all God's people were prophets!

Numbers 11.29

The rarest compliment the Church can pay a Christian is to describe him or her as a saint, but not far behind is the accolade that they are prophetic. There are men and women in the modern Church who are worthy to be named in the same breath as those Hebrew wild men of the Old Testament. They see things steady and see them whole while the rest of us thrash around treating the world like a cheap watch, to be subjected to inexpert investigation until all the pieces lie in front of us, defying our efforts to put them back together again.

But true prophets seem to be in such short supply that possibly Paul was right in regarding the prophetic office as a form of specialism – 'He called some to be apostles, some prophets, some evangelists, some pastors and teachers.' However, rightly or wrongly, throughout its history, the Church does not appear to have taken Paul very seriously. A man or woman called to the ministry has been expected to have a crack at all the jobs Paul catalogues, as well as others he'd never heard of.

There is New Testament support for rejecting the idea of prophecy as a rare specialism. That wry wish of Moses, 'Would that all God's people were prophets!' was granted a long time later at Pentecost when *all* present began to speak. From that time on, prophecy ceases to be the monopoly of a specialized elite within the Church and becomes an essential dimension in the witness of every Christian. And witness is the key word, for action is always superior to speech in the gospel, which is why the Word became flesh and not newsprint. Jesus was an amazingly tight-lipped prophet; for the most part he didn't tell people, he showed them.

To show people rather than to tell them requires a transformation of the prophetic personality. The old prophet was a talented individualist; the post-Pentecost prophetic spirit is expressed through a community of people in which hope has been made visible – a community whose spirit is so open, accepting and forgiving that no one with eyes to see can doubt that at least a bit of the old world has been changed into God's new creation.

Consider further this crucial distinction between prophecy in the Old and New Testaments. The Hebrew prophets were solitary, conscious of answering only to God himself for their words. From New Testament times on, the prophetic ministry is exercised within a framework of corporate discipline. The prophets were heard and then their words were put to the test by their fellows; as Paul told the church at Corinth, 'The spirits of the prophets are subject to the prophets.'

The great difference between old and new prophets was that *the* prophecy had been fulfilled, Christ had come as foretold in Scripture and so there was an absolute benchmark by which to test whether any prophet spoke truly. Was what was said consonant with the spirit of Christ; did it illuminate his life and teaching?

Prophets were also put through a rigorous test because in the community of faith, bursting with new life, there was always the danger of over-excitement being mistaken for rapture.

How, then, did the early Church put prophetic speech to the test? The oldest and most reliable method was that proposed by Jesus himself: 'By their fruits you shall know them' – the prophet's character should match his or her words. God-thoughts that pass through the mind and fall off the lips yet leave no impress on the character are suspect. Though morality is not the same thing as religion, it is a fair assumption that any true religious insight ought to result in a deepening of personal morality. It is not always easy to judge whether someone has grown in piety, but it is usually apparent whether he or she is honest and truthful.

The popular conception of the prophet as an irreverent wild man who swings his axe at the root of the tree is far removed from Paul's insistence that the prophet is part of a ministry whose task is to edify the Church – to accomplish not a demolition but a restoration job. The prophet edifies the Church by helping to purify its mind, keep its conscience tender and to distil one overarching Christian purpose from its much speaking, praying and witnessing. As Isaiah put it, 'You shall build up the old waste places, you shall raise up the foundations of many generations and you shall be called the repairer of the breach, the restorer of paths to dwell in.'

I will ask you a question

Mark 11.29

Much is made in the Old Testament of the distinction between true and false prophets. In the modern Church one way of telling them apart is by their attitude to the Bible. False prophets treat the Bible as an idol; true prophets allow it to pose searching questions. True prophets recognize that the Bible is not a time capsule buried thousands of years ago and pre-programmed by God to bellow out infallible answers to any question history might throw up. The Bible is a slab of history; it records the totality of the life of a people lived out in the presence of God. Of course it contains some unequivocal commands, but more often it is concerned to pose inescapable questions which people of this or any age evade at their peril. And it is these questions which are the touchstone of its relevance.

God to Adam: 'Where art thou?'

Isaiah to his people: 'Why will this nation perish for disobeying God?'

Jesus to every Christian: 'Why do you call me Lord and don't do what I ask?'

Jesus to a sick woman: 'What do you want me to do for you?'

Paul at Lystra: 'Why do you put your trust in gods that cannot save?'

According to my concordance, Jesus began a statement with a question no fewer than one hundred and sixty times. And these are special, urgent questions because they demand not academic answers but personal responses. God's word is in the questions because he treats us as responsible human beings, giving us scope for creativity in seeking the answers. He does not reduce us to mindless megaphones, passing on to our fellow human beings messages broadcast from a transmitting station beyond the stars.

Of course, those who treat the Bible as a compendium of pre-programmed answers to every question the human condition can throw up are able to make holy Scripture say virtually anything if they choose their text with care; for totally un-censored, the Bible tells the story of the writers' struggle to discover more about him.

Sometimes the biblical writers got it right and at other times they didn't, so you'll find within the Bible some of the most sublime human thoughts about God ever recorded, and pas-sages which, frankly, it is best to draw a veil over – as for example when the psalmist praises those who punish God's enemies by dashing their little children against rocks or when God allows whole communities to be massacred, or slaughters them himself through plagues, fire from heaven and other means. For example, God tells Saul: 'Smite Amalek and utterly destroy all they have and spare them not, but slay both man and woman, infant and suckling, ox and sheep, goat and ass.' Then, in a fury, he complains that Saul has not been ruthless enough; God can hear the bleating of a few animals whom the king has spared. Little wonder a Christian as orthodox as John Wesley could write that there are certain parts of the Old Testament that are not fit to be read in public.

Unless you are to treat the entire Bible literally as the word of God, you have got to judge the lowest by the highest, and in the Old Testament you can't get any higher than the portrait of God painted by the prophets. When one of them writes that what God desires is that we should do justly, love mercy and walk humbly with him, that is self-evidently true not just in a dim tribal past but anywhere at any time.

For Christians, the chief value of the Bible is that from its pages steps Jesus, who has been described as the human face of God; and therefore anything we read in the Bible which is alien to his Spirit we should treat with caution.

There is a huge issue here. The most explosive religious divide is not between adherents of one religion and another, or between those who have a religion and those who don't, but between extreme fundamentalists in any religion who demand blind obedience to the letter of some nailed-down truth and reject scholarship, and those who believe they are required to love God not just with their hearts and souls but also with their minds.

If there is a dearth of true prophecy in the Church it may be because we have treated the world as a captive audience – to be lectured, exhorted and damned. It is from the answers we return to the questions the Bible poses that the raw material of prophecy is fashioned.

I gave your ancestors no new commands about burnt offerings or other sacrifices when I brought them out of Egypt

Jeremiah 7.22

There is a popular notion that the essence of prophecy is novelty, daring new concepts of religion; that the prophet is free to say whatever comes into his or her head because the rule book has been discarded. In fact, the Old Testament prophets were not in the business of founding a new religion but of calling the people back to the purity of the old one. They were not concerned to be fashionable; when they parted company with their co-religionists it was with deep regret, not adolescent glee. True prophets were not like Cromwell's soldiers, rampaging through the monasteries, having an enjoyable time smashing sacred things. They constantly insisted they were in the direct line of succession to the mighty patriarchs, Abraham, Isaac and Jacob.

So too the Christian tradition, stretching back to the Apostles, is not to be brushed carelessly aside. To turn one's back on what the Reformers called 'Scripture and the Fathers' is no light thing.

The tradition is like a landmark in the desert so that the prophet who launches bravely into the unknown can find his way back if he gets hopelessly lost. Thus, some of God's greatest servants may have struck out into the dark but always kept one eye on the lights of home twinkling behind them. To the end of his life Martin Luther referred to the Church of Rome from which he had parted company as his 'Holy Mother', and John Wesley insisted throughout his differences with the Anglican Church that he was a loyal son of the Church of England. Even the most radical prophet recognizes that there are turbulent times when it is the very rigidity of tradition which holds things together.

Prophets are not anarchists; they are radicals – as the word implies, they desire to get to the root of the matter. They are radical in two senses – in their desire to get down to the very core of faith, and also in their firm grounding within that faith. And it is for this reason that they feel free to challenge it. Contrary to the popular meaning of the term, prophets are true traditionalists. They are jealous for the truth, the heart of the tradition which they feel is in danger of being corrupted.

To call the prophets traditionalists makes them sound stiff, starchy, formal. In fact they were passionate about their religion. When Jeremiah describes his call, he uses a word the translators of the King James version found a little strong, so they substituted the word 'deceived' for 'seduced'. What Jeremiah actually wrote was: 'Lord, you seduced me and I was seduced; you are stronger than I am and prevailed.' The prophet was press-ganged; he was not so much chosen as overwhelmed. His excuses were brushed aside. His resistance was overcome by divine aggression.

Words of prophecy well up out of moral passion that can no longer be contained, and this from a source deeper than bad temper or heated dissent. They are like a volcanic eruption bursting out in fire and flame on a specific occasion. To ask where Jeremiah got his sermon in the temple from or how Amos derived the searing condemnations at Bethel is like enquiring where Mozart got the C Minor Mass from. There is a mysterious quality about all truly inspired utterance.

It is an explosive mixture of words and emotions that explains the moral absoluteness of truly prophetic utterance. There is no 'nicely calculated less or more' about the prophet's reasoning. He knows almost by gut instinct when God's law is being violated and cries out in pain as though what is an affront to God is like a sword-thrust.

On the whole, prophets don't spell out detailed plans and propose programmes of action. Precisely how the sinful present is to be transformed into a glorious future doesn't greatly concern them; if pressed for their practical proposals, they would say much the same thing as Jesus did when asked to intervene in a property dispute: 'Guard yourself from every kind of greed.' That's not a very practical response to a specific problem of ethics, but in true prophetic style it draws attention to a moral absolute.

The prophets sound unconvincing when they desert the moral high ground. Ezekiel preaching about the valley of dry bones is full of power and eloquence. Then he goes on to describe the domestic detail of the restored temple, and we know he is off prophetic ground. Prophecy is a passionate vocation.

The Lord spoke to Moses as a man speaks to his friend

Exodus 33.11

The prophets are a radiant testimony to one of the great characteristics of the Judaeo–Christian God. Prophecy was only possible because they served a talkative God. The essential tool of the prophetic craft was the spoken word, because from the beginning, according to the Bible, that is how God related to his creation. One of the most extraordinary verses in the Old Testament occurs in the book of Exodus: 'The Lord spoke to Moses as a man speaks with his friend.' This was the early morning of religion when, in the tribes surrounding the Israelites, devotees approached their gods either struck dumb with terror or daring to address them only through some sacred formula. Yet here is a description of Moses and God engaging in chatty conversation, an image taking familiarity to a point just short of blasphemy.

The Judaism of the Old Testament was the religion of the talkative God. No sooner do human beings emerge on the stage of history than God is haranguing them: 'And God said, "Adam, where are you?"' or 'He called Abraham by name and he replied, "Here I am."' 'Come, let us reason together' was God's invitation to Isaiah. 'Stand on your feet; I would talk with you', he told Ezekiel. And Jeremiah sneers that the gods of the heathen are like scarecrows in a cucumber field because 'they cannot speak'.

The Old Testament prophet was first and foremost a speaker, only secondarily was he a seer, and even when he had a vision, he was instructed to turn it into words. The Lord told Habakkuk, 'Write this vision; inscribe it on tablets that it may be read at a glance.' The prophets were not scribes, and writing was uncongenial to them. Only when they were given explicit orders did they use tablets and scrolls to set down divine truth. Passionate speech, not the considered essay, was their forte.

The talkative God carries on the habit into New Testament times. When people converse as friends, much of what they say is unrehearsed speech that comes from the heart without having been edited by the mind. That's how Jesus talked, with utter spontaneity. As he himself put it, 'The mouth speaks what the heart is full of.' Even the apparent contradictions in some of his sayings may be put down to the unrehearsed way in which he spoke.

Nowhere in the Gospels is there any record of Jesus retracting or even modifying what he had said somewhere else. He never admits to any second thoughts. And except on one occasion when he wrote with his finger in the sand – hardly a medium likely to preserve his words for posterity – he never put his thoughts into permanent form. Though his words have been preserved in the Gospels for almost two thousand years, he did not seem to speak as one who anticipated that people in some remote time and place might ponder his sayings.

And Jesus urged this same spontaneity on his disciples. Even if the crunch came and they were hauled before the authorities, they were told not to think out in advance a careful defence: 'When you are arrested and taken to court, do not worry beforehand about what you are going to say; when the time comes, say whatever is then given to you.' This advice was not an encouragement to slovenly thinking or rash speech but a plea that they should rely on the freedom of expression that issues from a pure heart, a clear conscience and burning convictions.

Jesus' chosen medium, then, was unrehearsed speech without literary ornamentation or oratorical flourishes. In fact, he warned his disciples against heaping up empty phrases 'as the Gentiles do'. As we noted earlier, the novelist E. M. Forster once attacked 'poor little talkative Christianity' but Christians didn't catch the habit of verbosity from their founder, who spoke briefly and to the point, in short stories, epigrams and, most eloquently, through silence.

The contrast between the brevity of the Gospels and the length of some philosophical works of the time might be explained as the difference between revelation and persuasion. One can go on arguing a proposition for ever, coming at it from first one direction then another, answering objections, quoting authorities, pleading for understanding. On the other hand, there is a take-it-or-leave-it finality about revelation. It needs no supporting arguments because its authority must be assumed. As the prophets said, the one who utters it has 'delivered his soul', there is nothing to be added to the truth he has been given.

With utter candour, the Gospels report that some of those who heard Jesus speak went away shaking their heads in bewilderment. The concern of his own family went beyond puzzlement into doubt about his sanity. 'He is beside himself!' they said and were all set to put him away in an asylum. John the Baptist must have been a shrewd judge of prophetic speech, yet he could not decide from all he had heard whether Jesus was or was not claiming to be the Messiah. And no matter how often Jesus warned the disciples of his impending death they were still astounded when it happened. The gospel may have been a speech event but it certainly was not easily accessible mass communication.

For Paul too the gospel was 'a speech event' even though he is best known to us as a letter-writer. He disavowed what he called 'lofty words' and 'eloquent wisdom' in spite of taking pride in citizenship of a great metropolis which counted rhetoric, the art of formal speech, as one of its supreme glories.

Paul often expressed his frustration at the physical distance which separated him for long periods from the Christian communities he was responsible for. Had he been content to be in contact with them by writing alone, geographical remoteness would have been no problem, but he chafes that he cannot look them in the eye and talk to them face to face. He is accused by critics in the church at Corinth of being two-faced; the Paul who visits and talks to them is a different man from the one who from a distance aims at them harshly worded letters.

There is a salutary lesson in all this in the era of the mechanized message – writing, print, electronic media – which is speech without speaker, image without presence, contact without personal engagement. We may hear and see the word of life, but we cannot touch it.

The mass-media we use to convey the gospel embody a paradox, they provide universal accessibility to people's homes and yet corporeal remoteness. We can tell millions of people about God's love without it necessarily costing us any more than an expenditure of a little time and technique. It is love at a distance – at the other end of a microphone, camera or printing press.

The talkative God challenges all notions of love at a distance. Real love, like cheap wine, doesn't travel well. It requires the living presence of the loving agent to express itself in its fullness. Perhaps it is fanciful, but I'd like to think that the Incarnation happened because even God found loving at a distance frustrating.

We are cleansed from every sin by the blood he shed for us

I John I.7

This is a theme I have always found personally difficult. Hymns about 'fountains filled with blood' and 'being washed in the blood of the lamb' have a lack of fascination all their own. This emphasis on the blood of Christ seems to be a throw-back to an eerie past when devotees in the most sacred moments of life felt constrained to kill something in order to get right with God. So I've always let my eyes slide over the word 'blood' and treated it as a euphemism for the death of Christ, as the New Testament itself sometimes does.

But, as P. T. Forsyth taught me, to exsanguinate the imagery of the New Testament, hymnody and the eucharistic liturgy is to be left with a very pallid theological landscape. Christ's blood is splattered across our Bibles and hymnbooks and books of offices. What about those words Wesley whispered shortly before his death, 'There is no way into the holiest except by the blood of Christ'? Or there is that fascinating statement by Pope John XXIII to the effect that Protestants have something to teach Catholics who tend to be devoted to the sacred heart of Jesus and the blessed sacrament but not to the precious blood by which Christ paid for our redemption.

Unless one holds the most mechanistic view of God's providence, it was a coincidence that the religious rituals and the punitive procedures of Jesus' time both involved the spilling of blood. One cannot conceive of God holding back the advance of technology in order to forestall more modern methods of execution which would sever the link between blood sacrifice and judicial death through the spilling of blood. Nor would it have mattered how much blood Jesus spilt, one drop or all of it.

Not even in the Old Testament at its most sanguinary is there any suggestion that the virtue is in the substance of blood or in the suffering that accompanies it. Indeed, it would not have mattered had Jesus been killed in some other way – electrocuted or hanged or, like Socrates, made to drink the hemlock; the symbolism would have changed, that's all. It *would* have mattered had he died in his bed full of years and honour or dropped dead of a heart attack. Everything turns not on Jesus' life having been taken from him, but on his laying it down; yet not simply as a martyr lays it down – there can be an element of wilfulness or even subtle egotism in that. It was not sacrifice *by* the self but *of* the self which was the key to Christ's death, as was the giving up of himself to death by moral violence, at the hands of wicked men in violation of God's law. Blood most certainly symbolizes that.

So the Apostles were inspired innovators who used powerfully the coincidence of religious ritual and judicial procedure to reinforce each other. Athanasius said crucifixion was appropriate because it is only on the cross that a man dies with his arms outspread. That is a preacher's truth rather than a dogmatic one, yet the Apostles made connections between the public manner of Christ's death and the moral and spiritual religion of the Old Testament at its best.

In the Old Testament, a blood sacrifice was given *by* God before it was given *to* him, which by analogy makes the energy behind atonement God's grace rather than his wrath – a truth which undermines all theories based on severity of punishment or degree of suffering. The material sacrifice must be an outward symbol of the offerer's self-giving, a surrender of the will. True sacrifice is an ethical rather than sacerdotal or mystical transaction. The appeal of Christ's blood is to my will in obedience or rejection, not to my feelings in sympathy or revulsion.

The cross is not about God accepting sacrifice but making it; not depth of agony but height of surrender is its key. Christ confessed the holiness of God with his blood, for it is blood which sustains the central citadel of the human will. When we say that we are cleansed from all sin by the precious blood of Christ we are stating not just a truth about our personal redemption but about the transformation of the human condition. In this sense the garish imagery is justified: we *are* washed whiter than snow by the blood of Christ because the possibility of Christian perfection is ours.

With one exception, Jesus speaks only about his blood at the end of his life; for the rest he spoke of forgiving grace, but that was not possible for the world without judgement and sacrifice. The theory of the divine atonement which emphasizes the revelation of God's love or the call to repentance has its truth, but it is inadequate unless there is struck this note of judgement to do with sin, righteousness and a new creation.

The most powerful cultural force in the creation of civilization has been the metaphor. Without figurative expression, language would have been barren, the imagination starved and poetry impossible. Shorn of its metaphors and figurative speech the Bible would be in tatters, the teaching of Christ pedestrian. And of all metaphors, this one, 'The precious blood of Christ', is supreme; it has done more to change the course of history than any other. So I may sing and preach and pray about the blood of Christ without embarrassment or qualm for I am not wallowing in emotion but celebrating a wonder: Christ entering wounded into eternal life (remember Charles

Wesley's glorious line, 'The dear tokens of his passion, still his dazzling body bears'), in order that our eternity might be whole.

———◆———

Do you despise the Church of God?

I Corinthians 11.22

Well, in certain moods, I certainly despair of it – of its parochialism, its blindness to the signs of the times, its timidity, its petty snobberies, its Pharisaism; the sheer boredom and routine of much of its life. I know about such things because I have added to the sorry list by my own sloth and carelessness. Yes, I'd have to plead guilty. And I'm not alone. I have a library bursting at the seams with books which, whatever their titles, confirm that there are a thousand things wrong with the Church.

There *are* a thousand things wrong with the Church, but there is one thing right with it. It *is* the Church; it isn't a club or an institution or a society, an interest group, a lobby or a sociological entity. If it were, it would have gone out of business, been wound up, withered on the vine, crumbled into ruin long ago.

We are nervous of talking about what is right with the Church because we don't want to pander to the complacency of Christians. I have to say I've not noticed much complacency around in the modern Church. If anything, we go to the other extreme and whip ourselves with scorpions for our failure and inconstancy; our prayerlessness; the poverty of our worship and service; our lacklustre giving; our inability to communicate the gospel effectively in our generation. Smug? Self-satisfied? We spend most of our time not lauding it over our society but getting up off our knees to have another go at the job God keeps on entrusting us with, even though we go on making a hash of it.

Let's be unfashionable and celebrate what's right with the Church. We must begin with its foundation; with Jesus, 'the Author and finisher of our faith' as the letter to the Hebrews puts it. That has got to be the right foundation.

The Church is prior to all else in Christianity. There is a popular misconception of the history of Christianity which suggests that groups of early Christians, having read the Gospel accounts of Jesus, decided to form themselves into congregations at Rome and Corinth and Ephesus rather as supporters of Elvis Presley establish themselves in fan clubs. In fact, the precise opposite is the case. The Church did not come out of those accounts of Jesus' life we call the Gospels; the Gospels came out of the Church. They didn't establish the Church; the Church wrote them.

What we call the gospel is the Church preaching, theology is the Church thinking, worship is the Church addressing and being addressed by God, the New Testament is the Church remembering, mission is the Church helping God to enlarge the frontiers of the kingdom of heaven, the sacraments are the Church continuing the drama of the Incarnation. You cannot have Jesus without the Church because were it not for the Church we should know virtually nothing about him. No Jesus without the Church. His indwelling spirit is the essential cause of its consistent identity in every age and land and culture.

And the Church is in the right place. The ancient Greeks built their temples in sacred places, in the spot where God was felt to be present most intensely; where he was thought to reside. The scattering of the Christian Church higgledy-piggledy across the landscape proclaims the very reverse, the majestic truth that God is wherever we happen to be, not just in the great cathedral but in the tin tabernacle.

The Church is not more evidently to be found in its magnificent bastions than anywhere else. It is also there in its grandeur and misery at St Gertrude's by the gasworks with its peeling paint and leaking roof, its organ perpetually out of tune and its central heating perpetually out of commission. The Church's power and authority are not functions of its size nor the splendour of its buildings.

We sometimes talk about the Church in general as though it were a kind of ideal of which local churches are a partial and imperfect reflection. But the Church in general is an abstraction found in theological textbooks and on legal documents. There is no other church than the local church. That's what Incarnation means. The essence of Incarnation is locality.

We know from the Gospels that Jesus was a countryman with a rough tongue and a distinctive brogue. When Peter was caught out in the courtyard of Annas after the arrest of Jesus someone said to him, 'Your accent gives you away, you are one of them.' That puzzled gentleman Nathanael exclaimed a little snootily, 'Nazareth! Can anything good come out of Nazareth?' It was a village without prestige or sophistication and its inhabitants were regarded as country bumpkins. Could anything good come out of the little town, the local community? Nazareth was just a place, anywhere. But it is where our salvation sprang from and therefore it's where the Church too has its roots.

Where the Church exists at all, it exists in its entirety. If the one, holy, catholic and apostolic Church is not to be found where you are, it is not to be found anywhere. All its authority and duties and privileges fall to you. The Church is in the right place. For, like God, it is where we happen to be.

Jesus Christ, after whom the whole family in heaven and on earth is named

Ephesians 3.15

The Church has the right membership. Martin Luther said he wished that the word 'Congregation' had caught on rather than the word 'Church'. For him, a congregation was a gathering of those called together in answer to a summons. The Church gathers, not by accident or common taste or mutual agreement, but because they have been given the order to muster.

There is about any congregation the inevitability and haphazardness of a family. How does the author of Ephesians put it? 'Our Lord Jesus Christ after whom the whole family in heaven and on earth is named.' That's the Church, the whole family in heaven and on earth who name the name of Jesus. And we know how random a family is. You chose your friends, your partner, your enemies maybe your workmates even, but not your family. You're stuck with them.

The whole family on earth. Under the Church's banner marches, though they occasionally get out of step, the most extraordinary collection of disparate individuals, those who know and those who burn – mystics and militants; scholars and evangelists; priests and prophets; pacifists and crusaders; world-class thinkers and simple Bible believers.

The whole family in heaven. The struggle in which we are engaged is portrayed in the New Testament as cosmic in scope, and our earthly strength never seems equal to the task as we wrestle not against flesh and blood but against principalities and powers; so we need supernatural allies, and we have them in the Church triumphant. In assessing our resources, we must not ignore those regiments camped just over the hill. Think of that ascription which runs: 'Therefore with angels and archangels and all the company of heaven'. That is a formidable fighting force. And it is not just the giants of the Church who are camped over the hill, but those we have known and loved who worked and wept and prayed for the churches to which they gave their lives.

The Church has the right membership: anybody; anybody who has seen the light of the knowledge of the glory of God in the face of Jesus Christ. And it has the right message.

Two questions preoccupy all thinking people: why is the world the way it is; why are we the way we are – and what can be done about both? One is a question about history, the other about human nature. These questions recur in a thousand different forms and our proud society which has gone from complacency to utter impotence in a few decades hasn't the foggiest notion what to do about either. And they just happen to be the two questions the New Testament addresses. There is abroad in our day what might be called the 'Thought for the Day' syndrome: the Church ought to have something to say about *everything* and be able to say it in three minutes flat. The New Testament, however, is preoccupied with wholeness: how may the world be made whole, and how may I be made whole? The biblical word is salvation; it means the same thing.

How may this wholeness be achieved? This is the essential kernel of the Church's message. This is how Christianity, in a human sense, began – an extraordinary idea taking hold of a group of ordinary people and crying, 'Stand by me, believe in me; if necessary, die for me.' What is that extraordinary idea? Paul put it in a sentence: 'God was in Christ reconciling the world to himself.' That is the basic bedrock creed of the Christian Church, its message compressed to an irreducible minimum. The Church's entire existence, its essential genius, its distinguishing marks, the core of its theology, the theme of its Holy Book, the power of its preaching, the thrust of its ethics, the inspiration of its sacramental life, the justification for its mission – all hang on that one majestic reality: God in Christ reconciling the world to himself; making it whole, making us whole. That's the business we're about.

That's the right message, and it is just as well because it is the only message we are authorized to deliver; this is the one thing we ought to know more about than anyone else on earth, because we are in the salvation business. For the rest we're as much at sea as most other thoughtful people – our views on politics or economics or world affairs are as sensible or as wrong-headed as anyone else's. But we can claim the unique authority for that message.

Truly, there are a thousand things wrong with the Church, but for all its faults it is the only guardian of a gospel without which humanity is lost.

ASPECTS OF FAITH

There was silence in heaven

Revelation 8.1

Those Christians are fortunate who have never had the sense that they are addressing an empty sky when they pray. Isaiah put it differently, 'Truly you are a God that hides yourself.' And many people in our day would add to Isaiah's complaint the comment 'And you've made such a good job of it that we haven't the foggiest notion where to look for you.'

Let's be clear what the problem is. By God's silence I do not mean those times when because of our doubt or faithlessness we have no sense of his presence. That problem, though difficult to cope with, is easy to understand. But the Bible proposes a more serious possibility: that God shuts up shop, as it were, and retires beyond the range of our voices, and from heaven there is only an unfathomable silence.

From one angle the Bible is the record of God's progressive revelation of himself, but this contrary puzzling theme also runs through it, illustrated by Isaiah's complaint. And he is not alone. We have noted earlier in this book Job's lament: 'O that I knew where I might find him!' The Israelites at the time of Jehoshaphat bemoaned the lack of prophets to show them where God was, and one after another the prophets cried in indignation, 'Why do you not answer when we call upon you?'

What might this mean? God's silence might be the silence of approval.

One day I saw this notice on the skid-pan of a police driving school: 'Advance confidently until the bell sounds to signal an error.' No bell; no problem. Silent approval. The same idea pops up in many areas of life. When I was young I used to play football, and the first rule I was taught ran, 'Always play to the whistle.' Even if you think the ball has gone over the line or there's been an infringement, keep on playing until the whistle stops you. Take the referee's silence for approval until he demonstrates otherwise.

Silent approval: this is how we grow and learn. A wise parent steps back and allows a child to take his or her first faltering steps; a good teacher doesn't lean over the shoulder of a pupil and say, 'Do it this way, do it that way.' A wise boss isn't always nagging her workers; she gives them space without intimidating them with her overwhelming presence.

Have you ever been to the cinema with someone who has seen the film before and insists on giving you a running commentary on it? 'Now you see that fellow's got a knife hidden in his pocket and when the butler comes in, though he's not really the butler at all, he's an imposter. You're going to love the next scene where the vicar gets done in!' Imagine a world where the divine author of this drama we call life insists on talking us through it. Where would the suspense, the surprise, the adventure be? What is the point of making people capable of dreaming dreams and giving them nothing to dream about? Why would God create us capable of doing great things and then not allow us the freedom to fail? Say to us there are no mountains to climb, no new symphonies to write, no more discoveries to make, and a light will go out in the human mind.

To be human is to reach for things beyond our grasp, or life isn't worth the candle. We are allowed to grow and develop and fulfil ourselves because we haven't a nagging God who stage-manages the whole operation. Even if he expressed approval, we would read into his tone of voice all kinds of things. What could that slight pause mean? Better he keeps silent and trusts us to get on with our lives.

God's silence can be an expression of his approval. And silence can be a form of communication. I used to think the term 'silent communication' was a contradiction in terms until my computer crashed and I lost all my punctuation marks – full stops, semi-colons, capitals. All I had was endless chunks of text, great streams of words, and I suddenly realized how important silence is in communication. For that's what punctuation marks are, symbols of silence: where you pause, hesitate, ponder, take a breath.

All great artists are masters at speaking through silence – the object left out of the picture just where you'd expect it to be;

the void in architecture, the caesura, that pause in the middle of a line of verse; the note withheld in music. Recall, for instance, those four thundering 'Hallelujahs!' at the climax of the 'Hallelujah Chorus' – three of them, and then a pause that seems to last for ever, and then the crashing fourth. And in the throbbing silence is an unspoken 'Hallelujah!' as piercing as the others.

Many of the profound things that happen to us happen in silence. I once heard a German Christian talking about being at a bus stop in 1937 when the Gestapo came along and took a Jew out of the queue behind her and made him stand on his own. Someone asked, 'What did you do?' She replied, 'I didn't know what to do, so I just went and stood by him silently.' You could preach a dozen sermons against anti-Semitism and not reach that level of eloquence. Silent communication.

But how do we know it's the silence of communication? Suppose heaven is silent because it is empty? Well, in everyday life you know the difference between dead and living silences. You go into a restaurant and see two couples at adjacent tables and both are silent, but there is all the difference in the world between the two forms of silence. In one case the silence is a void, and in the other it is filled with presence. In one case, they are silent because they have nothing left to say and in the other they are silent because they have passed beyond the need for words. You know the difference between living and dead silence, because unless you've been amazingly lucky in your relationships you've been there.

On Calvary, when the redemption of the world was accomplished, Jesus spoke just seven words. Even heaven went silent. According to the book of Revelation, as the drama of our redemption reached its climax, 'there was silence in heaven for a space'. It is as though all heaven and earth held its breath to see whether this deed would be done. St John of the Cross said that throughout eternity God has spoken only one word, and that word is Jesus his Son.

The Lord turned and looked on Peter.
And Peter knew

Luke 22.61

Recall those terrible words in the letter to the Romans, 'There-fore, God gave them up.' He didn't hurl thunderbolts at them or strike them down, he merely left them to their own devices. Silent judgement. You see the same thing expressed after Peter has betrayed Christ. The text in Luke 22 runs, 'And the Lord turned and looked on Peter. And Peter knew.' No need for words. After all, if confronted by God's truth, if we don't know deep down where we are at and what we have done, then not even God himself thundering denunciation from heaven will make any difference. He may terrify us, but he won't change us.

Thomas Carlyle said, 'God sits in heaven and does nothing.' A lot of people think that. Because God is not booming at us from a transmitting station beyond the stars, we therefore assume the universe is in a state of anarchy. For us, noise means activity, and silence suggests passivity. It is understandable why people think that, but it is wrong.

One of the great themes of the Bible is the notion of a silent power in the universe which works retribution on evil. The Greeks believed in a goddess called Nemesis whose task it was to ensure that the evil got their just deserts. There is also a principle of retribution in Scripture. It is not a blind, irrational force; it is the irresistible outworking of a moral order vested in the holiness of God. The forces of gravity are silent, but if you buck them, you will pay for it. The moral order operates in silence, but if we buck it we suffer. 'Why do you kick against the pricks?' God asks Saul on the Damascus road. Why do you try to live and move and have your being against the rub of the universe?

It is Tertullian again making what seems to be that astound-ing assertion that the soul is naturally Christian. It is, as the computer experts say, our default setting. The claim of Paul in Colossians is that the whole universe was created through and for Christ. God created the world for the kingdom; it is the grain of the universe, the way things are. Hence, 'Come, inherit the Kingdom prepared for you from the foundation of the world.' And to try things any other way is to buck the logic of inevitability, and that means judgement.

The Bible insists that God takes the forces of history and with them shapes the ends of history to bring retribution on evil. The great nineteenth-century German historian Mommsen said that after a lifetime of historical study he had come to the conclusion that history has a nemesis for every sin.

You may have noticed recently that one or two of our judges have been appearing on television. Apparently some of their judgements have been so puzzling that people want to understand the thought processes behind them. Now in order to understand the inner motivation of any judgement, it is necessary to get to know the judge, and one of the great leaps of faith in the history of religion and in the human understanding of God took place when a man called Abraham went before the judge of all the earth in fear and trembling to beg for the life of the inhabitants of Sodom. It is one of the great set-pieces of biblical drama. 'Suppose I can find fifty just men . . . ten . . . five.' Then the punch-line: 'Shall not the judge of all the earth do right?' Abraham is saying in effect, 'God, there are certain things even you cannot do because they would betray your own inner nature.'

Abraham discovered to his astonishment that behind the judge's stern expression was the agonizing countenance of a father, and the slightest rebuke of a father is more punitive than all the fiery condemnation of a judge. If God the divine judge were to speak we would be destroyed, but God the divine Father keeps silent and his sorrow melts hearts that iron bars could not break.

There is an urgent and topical postscript to this theme of God's silent judgement. There are times when God keeps silent and allows someone else to speak for him. Jesus said, 'Inasmuch as you have done it unto the least of these, you have done it unto me.' So in the cry of the hungry for bread, the downtrodden for dignity and the victim for justice, God keeps silence so you can hear their voice.

There is one other possibility – God's silence is that of expectancy. We've all been in a theatre amid clamour and chatter, then the moment when the curtain is about to rise approaches, and a sudden hush falls over the house. Something is about to happen. Or we come to the end of a long and embattled argument when we have lobbied the options back and forth, then the debate dies away, someone must adjudicate or pronounce. Or take that wholly wondrous TV show *Blind Date* which all we elitists dismiss as pure tat and watch in spite of it. The girl has to choose between three men unseen behind a screen. The audience have roared encouragement, offered hints, cheered on their favourite's answers. Then comes the moment of decision and the studio falls silent. An eloquent silence awaits the decision.

So God's silence. What might it be? It could be a vote of confidence, an urgent message, a sorrowful judgement or the anticipation of a decision. But which? You know.

All things work together for good
for them that love God

Romans 8.20

The belief that the lives of individuals and nations are the concern of a power higher and wiser than they are is what religion is about. A God who reigns but does not govern is of little value. If God does not act in the world he may as well not exist, so is the world a drifting iceberg or a steered ship? That is the key question.

For much of the time, the origins of evil and suffering are an intellectual problem only for believers who have to reconcile awful eventualities with any notion of a loving purpose directing things. For the generality, an earthquake, for instance, is at least conceptually a natural event of the same order though on a different scale from the falling of a leaf. It may cause enormous suffering, and that is a tragedy, but for both explanation and alleviation, the general public would look to the vulcanologist and civil engineer, not to the theologian.

Yet every now and again in human history something happens so catastrophic that even the most sanguine non-believer is shaken out of one thought-mode, the practical, into another, the metaphysical. The 1755 Lisbon earthquake, for instance, demolished not only most of the city but also that Enlightenment optimism based on the notion of a beneficent agency in nature which provides for the well-being of all creatures. That perished in the rubble – as was pointed out with some force both by sacred writers such as Wesley in his pamphlet 'Serious Thoughts Occasioned by the Late Earthquake at Lisbon' and secular ones like Voltaire in *Candide*.

So there are times when even non-believers find that the sheer scale, impact and destructiveness of the world in uproar forces them to ponder the illogical but clamant question: how could a God we don't believe in allow such things to happen? Inadvertently, they find themselves making common cause with believers wrestling with the challenge of reconciling catastrophe with God's loving purposes.

In our day it is the advent of broadcasting and particularly television which is forcing the general public to face such disturbing issues. By courtesy of live television a ravaged, violent world implodes into our living rooms. Instantaneously, as they happen, we see the bombs explode, the seas smash the barriers, the buildings crash, the starving children die before our eyes. We see evil rampant, in all its dimensions and variety, calamities both natural and of human contriving. As through a porthole into a seething boiler, we watch a creation in pain, convulsed by all those catastrophes which were once quaintly described in the old insurance policies as Acts of God. Non-believers may be philosophical about awful happenings attributable to sheer human wickedness, for they know they are no angels themselves. But there is about nature's violence not just huge destructiveness in terms of mortality and material devastation but also an added dimension of sheer irrationality which makes any thinking observer very uneasy.

God's providence is surely the conviction that the world in its tragedy and grandeur is unfolding as one great divine creative act. It is the confidence that all will be well in the end, not that his purpose is transparent in his willingness to do this individual act rather than that one at our earnest urging. Only in view of its final purpose does the world make any sense.

As in a world war, there are engagements on land, sea and in the air – some victories, some defeats, some stalemates. How could one judge the final outcome by a small skirmish in Burma or a great sea battle in the Pacific? How does the shooting down of one aircraft in this patch of sky or the death of a single soldier on that spot act as a pointer to final victory or defeat? In themselves, individual engagements may seem inconclusive or unintelligible, yet at some point they bear upon a single, great central issue, final victory or defeat. But in the heat of battle, who can sense the ultimate drift of things? Even the greatest statesmen and war leaders cannot always discern through the smoke and flame the bright goal beyond. Three months before the end of the First World War, Lloyd George was confiding to his diary that he feared all was lost.

To change the metaphor, we are like members of a fledgling orchestra playing a piece for the first time, but with this difference: because the composer is present, whatever mistakes we make are incorporated by her into the final score. We think we have complete freedom to extemporize, and so we have; yet every note we play is woven into a theme of the utmost complexity. As are sounds not of the orchestra's making. This is Tchaikovsky's 1812 stuff – not just violins but cannon; not just trumpets but rolls of thunder. And some of those sounds the composer incorporates into the score are dissonances of the most awful kind.

It was said of Mozart that often he didn't visualize his compositions note by note but as a whole. The theme was complete in his head before he set down a single note, and mathematically speaking there were endless combinations of notes that might have achieved his overall purpose. Lesser composers worry about how to get from one chord to the next. So do we. Our creativity is derivative and limited. Nevertheless, just as Mozart did not save up all the beauty and worth of an entire composition for its climax, each chord having its own inherent validity, so we trust there is meaning in our daily service even when we do not see how the notes for which we are responsible relate to the next.

If all things were made plain, we could trace the filaments of our influence in the new creation, all we are and have done and experienced which have withstood the refiner's fire. But we are caught between the old creation and the new; writes the author of the letter to the Hebrews, 'We do not yet see all things in subjection to him, but we do see Jesus.'

It is the cross which puts catastrophe in its true perspective, for the God who spared not his own Son will not scruple to bend the most dreadful eventualities to his purposes. God makes the forces that rage against him work to accomplish his ends. When we pray that God's kingdom come, do we really know what we are asking for? 'Theodicy' is the technical term for the defence of a loving God in the face of evil and suffering, and the only theodicy which makes sense is to be found in the cross. To redeem the world cost more than to create it. All the perverse energy of a world God has entrusted with freedom pulled on the knot Christ had to undo. This then was the world's supreme crisis, much more fearsome than any imaginable human catastrophe – earthquake, famine or sword.

The future can add nothing in principle to the great settlement of good and evil made on Calvary. There is nothing ahead of humanity that has not already been discounted in that encounter on Calvary. The key to history is not the answer to a riddle but the victorious outcome of a battle.

Because you did not know ...

Luke 19.44

The gospel is many things, one of them a body of truth, of saving truth. Some of Jesus' sternest words were directed at the citizens of Jerusalem as he wept over the city: 'There will not one stone be left upon another *because you did not know* the things that belong to your peace; your enemies will bring you and your children to destruction *because you did not know* God's time is here.'

There are things we ought to know, but don't. My grandmother's favourite saying was, 'What you don't know won't hurt you!' I soon learned that one isn't true when I tried to change a plug and forgot the new colour coding. I discovered that what you don't know can kill you.

Wallace Hamilton tells how, in 1881, President James Garfield of the United States was shot. This was before the era of the X-ray and doctors couldn't agree on the location of the bullet. His personal physician, Dr Bliss, said he was certain the bullet was in this spot; a specialist consultant Dr Weiss said no. While the doctors argued, the patient died. An autopsy proved Dr Weiss right. Whereupon the *Boston Globe* ran the headline: 'Where Ignorance is Bliss, tis folly to be Weiss.'

There is no area of human life where ignorance is bliss. During my years in Central Africa, it was not the poverty and hunger which oppressed me but that darkening of the human mind, those impenetrable shrouds of superstition and primitive mythology which made almost impossible sound cultivation and scientific husbandry and efficient irrigation.

What we don't know and ought to. Then there are the things we think we know, and don't.

Our local greengrocer had a sign over a box of apples that read, 'As English as St George!' I applauded his patriotism but doubted his accuracy. St George wasn't English; if he was an historical character at all, he was Libyan. Interesting, isn't it, the things we take for granted as true, and they turn out not to be?

We say, everybody knows . . . for instance, everybody knows Sherlock Holmes' famous dictum, 'Elementary, my dear Watson.' Well, he never said it. Not once. Though to prove it you'd have to plough your way through all the Sherlock Holmes books, which would call for the blood, sweat and tears Churchill urged on us during the war. Blood, sweat and tears? That's not what he said. It was 'Blood, toil, tears and sweat.' Almost the same, but not quite. And the difference would matter if you were a wordsmith like Churchill. For getting that wrong, you deserve the fate of Samson who, you will recall, had his hair, the source of his strength, chopped off by Delilah. Everybody knows that's what happened. Well, look up the original story in the book of Judges and you will discover that Delilah never touched Samson's hair. She sent for a barber.

It's all good, harmless fun for quiz purposes, but at a more serious level misinformation – the things we think we know and don't – spawns bigotry, which is about forming strong opinions without bothering to check our facts. Everybody knows that women drivers are terrible, that the Scots are mean, the Irish are drunks, the English are stuffy. Everybody knows that Christians are hypocrites, Jews are avaricious, Muslims bloodthirsty . . .

We say, 'Everybody knows.' Whenever someone begins a sentence with that phrase, it's a pound to a penny they don't.

Then there are the things we'd rather not know. When I worked for the BBC, the awful items our news bulletins contained were bad enough, but even more depressing was the reaction of members of the public who would phone in protesting that they didn't want their evening spoilt by news footage of starving babies in Ethiopia or refugees on the move in Kurdistan or homeless people sleeping under Waterloo Bridge. They'd say, 'We don't want to know: we've troubles enough of our own.'

One of the most evocative scenes in the Channel Four documentary series *The World at War* shows Hitler in his bunker surrounded by his generals, poring over a huge table-map of the Russian front. He moved symbols which represented German divisions from this point to that, and his generals stood by and watched impassively. Nobody dared tell him that none of those divisions existed. They had all been wiped out. Sometimes at church conferences I get the uncanny feeling we're going through the same exercise – moving divisions that no longer exist, living out strategies that died long ago.

Incarnation means that Christ lived in and died for this world. He came to redeem us, and he can redeem us from anything but illusion. Not even Christ can save a fantasy world. There is that pregnant phrase in the parable of the prodigal son: 'And when he came to himself . . .' Once he was back in the real world he was within the realm of redemption. Plato defined religion as an instinct for reality. Truth is a sort of map of reality we tamper with at our peril. That's what they tried to do in Stalinist Russia – bend reality to fit their maps of it. Tourists in Moscow would find themselves staring at a place of worship and then look down at the official map in their hands and find there was no trace of it. We may have to redraw our maps to accommodate our growing understanding of reality – the sciences are doing that all the time. But to do it the other way round and try to make reality fit our maps is insanity.

Then there are the things we cannot know.

One of the reasons I am a Christian is that Christianity explains more about me and about the world in which I live than any of its rivals. Its account of the glory and tragedy of human nature is more comprehensive than that of the humanist; the Christian doctrine of history as a complex interplay of good and evil is more profound than that of the Marxist.

Yet, though I find that the Christian faith explains more things than its rivals, it doesn't make the mistake of trying to explain everything. It is widely held that the light of scientific knowledge will increasingly dispel human ignorance until only a shrinking patch of darkness remains in which the things of God are hidden. On Isaac Newton's tomb are carved the words:

Nature and nature's laws lay hid from sight
God said, 'Let Newton be', and all was light.

But that's not what Newton himself said. He talked about seeing himself as a little child picking up pebbles on the beach while all around him was a vast unending sea of the unknown.

We can know only one thing about the unknowable – it is merciful. That is the united testimony of Bible and tradition and saints. There is no dark sinister force at the heart of things; no gaping black hole at the heart of the universe that swallows up our idealism and goodness and faith as though it had never been.

Which leaves what we absolutely must know – the one in whom we believe.

You are the image and glory of God

I Corinthians 11.7

Moses forbade the making of any graven images because these products of our hands and brains can easily become substitutes for the real thing – having created the idols of wood and stone we may never move on to true faith. Jesus was aware of this danger; according to the fourth Gospel, he warned his disciples, 'He who believes in me doesn't believe in me but in him who sent me.' Even he mustn't become an idol, a substitute for

Almighty God. And at various times throughout Christian history that is precisely what has happened – we have turned Jesus into an idol; the last time I suppose was in the 'swinging sixties'. The 'Jesus people' turned Jesus into an idol, just as some time before their idols had been the Latin American freedom fighter Che Guevara and Bob Dylan.

Moses' prohibition isn't just against any graven image of God but of anyone and anything in the heavens above or on the earth beneath – we are not just given to make graven images of God, thus diminishing him, but also graven images of our fellow human beings which are demeaning and distorting and undermine the mystery and complexity of the human personality.

The poet William Blake writes somewhere about the tyranny of mind-forged manacles, so that when we encounter certain groups or races we immediately call up a simplistic mental image in our minds; we've had one bad experience with them and so turn it into a general principle. Human beings become graven images.

And what is worse, we may not only be the victims of other people's image-making, but impose demeaning images on ourselves. I'm hopeless, I'm pathetic. I'm a failure. I'm too old, too dim, too poor. Mind-forged manacles. At some time or another most of us are imprisoned in them.

And this is where the Church comes in. It's as though the altar or communion table were a great anvil to which we come in order to have our mind-forged manacles struck off. The gospel is like a hammer which shatters the constricting images that imprison us. We can be free both of the images others impose on us or those we impose on ourselves, because the only image that matters is the image God has of us.

Which brings us to Paul's statement that we are the image and glory of God.

The image God permits us to have is not the work of our hands or brains; it is his achievement. Remember the psalmist: 'Thou has crowned us with glory and honour and made us just a little lower than divine.' Just a little lower! That must be the psalmist's joke. But it's still an impressive credential. The image and glory of God. That's us.

Now at this point I get cold feet. I have an uncharacteristic attack of modesty. Me, made in the image of God? If so, he must be a very nondescript deity because I'm a very nondescript specimen of humanity. But even if I weren't, even if I were a paragon of virtue, a moral giant, I'd still be a speck in the solar system; therefore if I am the image, then the reality must be pretty unimpressive. It is understandable I should think that, but it isn't true.

As a matter of sober fact, I am not a paltry bit of creation, nor are you. If you take everything that went into our making, we represent a huge investment on God's part. Billions of years of evolutionary pain, to start with. Countless species went to the wall so that we might emerge to fulfil our human destiny. God couldn't make me, just me, without making a whole world as well, because the scientists say life emerged from the sea as a speck of tissue, and that bit of matter is the point of an enormous pyramid, for what did it take to produce that ocean? A giant interlocking system of atmosphere and tides and sun and moon – all conspiring to create that life-bearing blob which became me.

So pardon my presumption. I may be a little moth-eaten, a little battered at the edges, but even science agrees that I am an extraordinary work of nature. A little lower than divine. And the New Testament goes even further. The proof that we are made in God's image is that he found it possible to come among us and share our nature – the Word became flesh, the divine Word wrapped itself in this frail wayward stuff that enshrines our personality.

All that's fine in theory, but how does the theory become reality? Through that process of transformation we call Christian regeneration or conversion – which may happen in an instant or take a lifetime. This is the way in which we are conformed into the image of Christ.

'Conversion' is a word which causes great embarrassment in certain parts of the Church. I've never understood why. People in our society are getting converted to and from one thing and another, ranging from coal gas to natural gas, from pounds to euros, Manchester United to Manchester City, the Labour Party and the Liberal Democrats, all the time. It is a perfectly natural phenomenon. But the image that religious conversion conjures up is of sharp-nosed fanatics exuding clouds of superheated piety stalking society, thumping people on the back and demanding to know whether they have been saved. Yet why should it be thought odd for someone to be converted to an acceptance of the Christian faith as a result of the impact made on him or her by the person and teaching of Jesus?

And this is what conversion means – not a bout of self-indulgent soul-tickling but a sustained act of will, the ultimate result of which is radical character change. For this is the acid test of conversion – not primarily the effect it has on a person's prayer life or Bible reading (you'd expect it to change them), but what change it makes at the pressure points of our lives; and the pressure points of our lives have to do with our attitudes to money, ambition, power, justice, race and the like. If conversion does not affect them, then it is not conversion as the New Testament understands it.

So conversion is the process whereby a captive personality is liberated by the power of the person and teaching of Jesus. This is how, as John's Gospel promises, we are 'given the power to become . . .', to take off in quite unexpected new directions. There's nothing unexpected about the direction in which our hatreds, fears and aggressions will take us – we have been there before. But nobody knows what the love of God in Christ might do. This is the power that smashes off mind-forged manacles, that shatters vicious circles of cause and effect, and liberates us. This is what Paul is talking about – not the graven image of an invisible God but a living image of Christ.

This is a word people need to hear in a society which tends to depersonalize us. We matter; we don't exist to be counted, we count. We have cosmic dignity. This is what we need to remember in our moments of loneliness, self-denigration or despair. We are not naked apes, or handfuls of dust or evolutionary accidents or specks on a planet floating in outer space or a sixteen-digit number on a computer card. According to the first epistle of John, '*Now* are we the children of God and it does not yet appear what we shall be.' We have an open future. It is our cosmic destiny to be the image and likeness of Christ. All we have to do is accept it.

You thought God's gift was for sale

Acts 8.20

The Victorian preacher C. H. Spurgeon describes how he went with money from his church collection to help pay the rent of a poor woman of the parish. He knocked again and again but failed to get any response. The woman was inside, but she didn't open the door because she thought it was the rent man. The knock signalled a gift; she thought it was a demand.

Religion begins with a gift, the gift of seeing, not a demand, the demand to prove God's existence. That is to start from the wrong end with dogmas and definitions. Cardinal Newman, who was a considerable theologian, said of the classical proofs for the existence of God, 'They do not warm me or enlighten me; they do not take away the winter of my desolation or make my moral being rejoice.'

We can't turn definitions into living experiences. We can study musical theory until we are blue in the face, but unless the penny drops when we hear music, we may as well have a tin ear. Art doesn't begin as an exercise in proving the existence of beauty; it's when we encounter a work of art and the penny drops that we start to have thoughts about what beauty is.

It is as futile to approach religion from the angle of theology as to study a rose from the angle of the Special Theory of Relativity. Theology follows from religious experience, it rarely triggers it. We don't first decide what a being called God is like and then look around for someone who deserves the title. First comes that sense of strangeness, of awe or reverence, then we try to put words round our experience.

When this happens, everything seems different for those worn down on the treadmill of dull religious observance. Familiar words in hymn and Bible burst into flame and the commonplaces of the Creeds grow astonishing. God seems real, there. Religious believers have made the discovery that reality is not just what happens to be there; it is something we have been given, and givenness hints at another word, grace – that which is freely offered out of God's self-expression.

How do we get the point about religion? Rarely as a result of sitting down with a towel round our heads and reflecting upon Life, the Universe and Everything. It's not usually the final link in a chain of logical argument. More likely we're scanning the often barren landscape of our lives, and some feature that has been there all the time suddenly stands out in sharp relief. As the phrase goes, our attention is caught; the truth beckons us. The penny drops.

These penny-dropping experiences can happen anywhere and at any time. Thomas Merton, the twentieth-century Trappist monk, was reading a letter written by the poet Gerard Manley Hopkins to Cardinal Newman. And 'Suddenly,' he wrote, 'something began to stir in me, something began to push, to prompt me. It was a movement that spoke like a voice.' Bede Griffiths, the Anglican monk, first experienced what he called 'transcendent illumination' as a schoolboy. Later, he wrote this about the penny-dropping experience: 'It could come through nature or poetry, or through art and music, or it could come simply through falling in love or through some accident or illness – anything which breaks through the routine of life may be the bearer of this message to the soul.'

One of the most famous of all modern penny-dropping experiences occurred in 1926. C. S. Lewis wrote, 'I was going up Headington Hill on the top of a bus. Without words and (I think) almost without images, a fact about myself was presented to me. I became aware that I was holding something at bay, or shutting something out. I felt myself being given there and then a free choice. I could open the door or keep it shut.'

Now, these penny-dropping experiences may fall a long way short of what a religious person means by conversion. C. S. Lewis insisted that when the penny first dropped, the God to whom he surrendered was, in his own words, 'sheerly non-human'. Rarely do those who have these experiences see the outlines of the Nicene Creed flashing across the sky or hear God's voice calling their name and tapping them on the shoulder as a friend might do. That can happen, but more usually it is the intensification of the normal rather than a visitation from the supernatural which has someone exclaiming, 'Of course! How blind I've been!'

One thing is sure: when the penny does drop, those right outside the circle of formal religion begin to doubt their negative certainties. And for those worn down on the treadmill of dull religious observance, everything seems different.

That is not evidence our common sense should ignore. The proof is all round us. Religious believers have seen something, and what they have seen has changed them. And it is a gift; we don't buy it by laboured effort or tortured religious observance. Said Paul, 'The gift of God is eternal life through Jesus Christ our Lord.'

The trumpet shall sound and the dead shall be raised

I Corinthians 15.52

Let us celebrate the spiritual power of music. Christianity began with passionate preaching and left in its wake theology, the propositions of religion, the cold dogmas of the textbooks. And how did the Church bring them to life again? By setting them to music. I once heard a radical theologian asked if, in the light of all he had written, he could honestly say the Apostles' Creed? He said, 'No, but I can sing it.' We can sing beyond our conscious beliefs because the sheer power of music sweeps up and transcends our doubts and agnosticism.

Music is the language of affirmation. It is hard to say 'No' to a truth set to great music. Here's a choir thundering out the 'Dies Irae' of one of the great Masses. Stop them and ask 'Do you believe all that about God's Awful Judgement Day?' and you'd get a variety of answers ranging from 'Absolutely!' through 'It's just figurative, isn't it?' to 'I love the music!'; but set the choir going again and together they'll express in music a greater truth than many of them dare acknowledge individually in words.

This is the secret of the power of great hymns. Confront the average person with those sonorous phrases in the Nicene Creed, 'Very God of very God, begotten not made, being of one substance with the Father' and he or she will say, 'Oh, all that philosophical stuff's beyond me'; but give them Charles

Wesley's Christmas carol, 'Hark, the Herald Angels Sing' and they will bellow away, 'Veiled in flesh the Godhead see, Hail, the Incarnate deity.' That's high theology brought alive to the sound of the trumpet.

What words make clear, music brings alive. I was born and bred in the Lancashire brass band and choral society tradition – and I can't hear the phrase 'The Trumpet shall sound' without being transported back to performances of *Messiah* at the Victoria Hall, Bolton, when I was young. At that time I was going through all the usual adolescent stages of agnosticism, exploring the frontiers between faith and unfaith, wandering far away from the centre. But like a bugle call summoning the scattered ranks of an army, at the first notes of 'The Trumpet shall sound', I was back on parade.

Music explodes buried time-bombs in the mind. Walt Whitman wrote, 'Music is what awakens in us when we are reminded by the instruments.' For a number of years I was Head of Religious Television at the BBC and one of the programmes for which I was ultimately responsible was *Songs of Praise*. The general view in the television service was that it was long past its sell-by date. Society had moved on, church attendance was shrinking, our society had become more deeply secular. But what baffled the pundits was that the ratings of *Songs of Praise* remained firm, and in times of crisis or trouble rose dramatically.

It was that time-bomb effect. Many people learn hymns as children, sing them at school, hear them at weddings and funerals, then they drift away from church, life moves on and these images sink to the bottom of the memory. Deep down there, they slumber on and then along comes some crisis or the desire to celebrate or the need for comfort. And there, deep in the subconscious are the precise words needed as expressed by the great hymnodists. And what often brings the words to the surface is the tune. Hum the tune and the words come back to you.

Time-bombs in the mind detonated by music: I recall leaving Oxford in the 1950s to go off to be a missionary in central Africa. On a glorious summer's afternoon I walked through a leafy square on the way to the station to get the train for Southampton and then the Union Castle boat to Cape Town.

From an open attic window in the square came the strains of Vaughan Williams' *Variations on a Theme by Thomas Tallis*. And on a number of occasions in the years that followed, I found myself in turbulent, even violent times; but I only had to hear that theme and I was reminded that life is not all hunger and war and strife, it has a gentleness and beauty and peace too.

Music doesn't just bring our past experience alive: in it is prefigured our future. There is music in our soul because there is music in God. How do we know that? It is a matter of logic. Because we have been made in the image of God, we would expect to find perfectly realized in him any qualities and faculties we human beings demonstrate at our highest and best; and at our highest and best we make music. Hence, it is hard to conceive of a tone-deaf God. Indeed, Karl Barth wrote that when he got to heaven he would expect to hear the music of Bach being played on all the great formal occasions, but when the heavenly host was relaxing it would be to the strains of Mozart.

When we call music a universal language, we don't just mean that it overleaps national boundaries and unites those whom words divide; it also reaches out into that gulf between time and eternity, earth and heaven. That's why great music often fills us with a sense of yearning: it brings us to the very edge of a totally uncharted dimension of existence which eludes us – the music goes where we cannot follow because we are earthbound.

Spiritually, this sense of yearning which music can evoke could be called homesickness. We are all exiles, like the prodigal, on a journey from the far country to the Father's house. Remember the psalmist crying, 'How shall we sing the Lord's song in an alien land?' Great music sharply reminds us of what we are missing, for it is the mother tongue of heaven.

Cast an eye on that strange last book of the Bible, the book of Revelation: it's an attempt to do the impossible and put into words what the end of all things will be like, when there is a new creation, a new heaven and earth, when the love, peace and joy of God's kingdom will be universal. The author St John the Divine does his best to find the vocabulary to describe this vision, but whenever he is totally overwhelmed and he doesn't know how to express the glory and joy of it, he brings on the trumpets and choirs. Trumpet blasts resound through heaven as angels announce the abolition of all the great scourges that have plagued humanity – war, wickedness, famine; choirs of angels sing antiphonally of the glory of God.

But we are not there yet. Like the people of Israel, we are still plodding through the wilderness; but to encourage us on our way, we have music, the dialect of our homeland to give us melodies to march to and songs to cheer our spirits and the occasional bugle blast to keep us awake until we arrive at journey's end.

What is the point of all this sacrifice? (Remembrance Sunday)

Isaiah 1.11

Every year, the Remembrance Day commemoration becomes more problematic. Its origins, of course, lie in that vast blood-letting of 1914–18, now fading further and further into the past – and fewer and fewer of the heroic survivors of that historic conflict remain. An increasing number of generations separate us from the Second World War. The two so-called world wars, for all their confusions and historical complexities, could be understood in some sense as titanic battles of good against evil. The conflicts which have followed have been more morally ambiguous; the rights and wrongs have not been as easy to identify. Service personnel and civilians bled and died in Korea, the Falklands, the Gulf War and Iraq; and God knows, they are equally deserving of remembrance and the nation's gratitude. But these were not wars about which, if we are honest, the nation felt entirely comfortable.

And, of course, the greater number of British servicemen and women who have died in action over the past twenty years fell not in some corner of a foreign field but on home ground in a province of the United Kingdom called Northern Ireland. When is a war not a war?

So the memories grow dim and the moral issues become more blurred. Ought we not then to call it a day and allow relatives and friends to commemorate fallen loved ones privately, in their own way? For three reasons I think not.

First, because as a nation we made certain promises to those who served and died, and occasions like this force us to remember those promises.

My father was a Lancashire coal miner who served in the trenches throughout the First World War and was severely wounded on the eve of the Armistice. As a small child in the Depression of the early 1930s, I recall watching him sitting by the fire, unemployed, gazing into the flames and saying bitterly, 'They promised us a land fit for heroes to live in!' And we did. Read the literature. That was one of the political slogans of the time – a land fit for heroes to live in. The other was this: it was to be a war to end all wars. That's what unnumbered men died in the mud believing.

Both promises were broken. The survivors came back to slump and depression and unemployment. And the seeds were already being sown of yet another war.

And the political rhetoric of the Second World War was also laden with promises about a new deal, making the world safe for democracy and the ridding of the old class divisions in a welfare state where all the public services on which the community's life depended would not be at the mercy of the market but backed by national resources.

Promises, promises. From time immemorial, promises to the dying have had a sacred and binding significance. Whoever takes up arms in war is potentially writing off his or her life. If you ask someone to risk everything in a cause by assuring them that this cause will affect their destiny and that of generations to come, then you've got to honour your promises. If things stay just the same when the shooting stops and people begin to forget what it was all for, then there has been a betrayal of the sacred dead.

This truth imbues politics with a new urgency and significance. Every time a politician, whether national or local, passes a war memorial he or she must recognize that the future for which they sincerely strive, whatever their party allegiance, has been paid for in blood. Every voter on the way to a polling booth would do well to realize that the simple act of putting a cross against a name on a ballot paper is a privilege that has been bought by someone's life.

That's one reason why we must remember. And here's another. War is always a confession of humanity's failure. Armed conflicts are productive of extraordinary courage, sacrifice, endurance and comradeship; but at root, when nations must resort to mass killing to defend their interests, somewhere there has been a failure – in wisdom and magnanimity and far-sightedness or even in plain common sense.

What a doleful tale history tells. In the past hundred years, younger generations found themselves having to fight and die to destroy the monsters that their elders had created. A study of history will show that the roots of the two great wars of the twentieth century are to be found in a victorious Britain at the end of the Napoleonic Wars so convinced that France would always be the great enemy that we insisted on fortifying and building up Germany. And a few decades later, the sons of those British statesmen died in their thousands to slay the monster we helped to create. One root of the Second World War lay in the severity of the reparations the victorious Allies demanded from a devastated and unstable Germany. Decades later, it suited the West's book to build up Saddam Hussein's Iraq to neutralize our perceived enemy Iran, with the result that British troops ended up dying from bullets and shells supplied by Western armament manufacturers.

And so it goes on. The glorious allies of one war become the evil and vicious enemies of the next. Now, it is easy in retrospect to see the failings and shortcomings of the world's statesmen. But one of the lessons history teaches is that in an international crisis there is sometimes a critical point at which a dangerous situation can be resolved before catastrophe supervenes. In the moulding of metal there is a moment when it is neither too soft nor too hard to be shaped at will. But let the temperature drop or rise by a few degrees and it's too late. In just the same way, there is a tide in human affairs, a moment that can be seized before things slide into disaster, a point at which we still have the initiative, where we are one jump ahead of events. If we miss that moment of truth which is a time for forgiveness, magnanimity and farsightedness, then attitudes will harden, wounds unhealed will fester, an unrepeatable opportunity will be lost. Then there is an awful inevitability about the future.

So we need Services of Remembrance to remind us just what stakes we are playing for on the world stage. People have paid dearly for our obstinacy, greed, incompetence and desire for revenge.

War confronts us, on the largest possible scale, with death as one of the abiding realities of our existence. Twenty million Russians, five million Germans, three million Japanese and half a million Britons and Commonwealth citizens died between 1939 and 1945. Death is all around us as a fact of our existence, but war brings us face to face with that raw reality on a scale from which we cannot escape. Those endless rows of neat white crosses or elegant memorials bring us up sharp against one of the great challenges to religious faith. Where are they now?

Most thoughtful people are at some time or another oppressed by the tragic absurdity, the prodigality with which we expend life. Billions of years of evolutionary pain, the endless, slow evolutionary march of sentient life, generation upon generation is halted, wiped out even, by a stray bullet or an exploding bomb.

It is the deathless power of God's love in investing our lives, whoever we are, with eternal significance which led the Russian philosopher Berdyaev to claim that every human soul has more value and meaning than the whole of history with its empires, wars and revolutions. Every one of those names carved in stone on fading war memorials is greater than the epic battles and mighty conflicts and grand strategies in which he or she seemed to be a tiny component. That's why we remember the fallen in churches like this, in the presence of God. To keep our priorities right. Any of those thirty million people who died in the Second World War counts for more in the balances of God than the world-shaking events which occupy chapters in the history books.

What does it say on the war memorials? 'Their names live for evermore.' Sadly, it's not true. The weather and the passage of time slowly erode those names; generations pass by who have never heard of them. No, it's not their names that live for ever: they do. That we declare on the authority of the gospel.

So we remember the glorious dead with gratitude, in penitence and supremely with the assurance that God does not merely remember them but enfolds them eternally; that the awesome dark beyond our gaze is filled not with nothingness but with his love.

Why do you want to know my name?

Genesis 32.24–30

The story is one of the earliest forms of communication, and here is a story bursting with insights about our attempts to get in touch with God. Jacob wrestles all night with an unknown adversary by the ford at the River Jabbok. One tradition identifies the stranger as an angel; another suggests that Jacob's adversary is God himself in human form; a third said it was a man, though the Old Testament scholar Gerhard von Rad writes, 'the word "man" is open to the widest possible interpretation'. Whichever tradition is preferred, Jacob's opponent is the embodiment of divine communication.

By the time the sun rises and Jacob's opponent leaves him, several things have happened. He has a fresh sense of his own identity, symbolized by a new name, Israel; he thinks he knows who his adversary is, and he has been crippled in the struggle. Divine–human communication in this story is achieved not as a dialogue between philosophers but as a wrestling match between opponents; a close encounter rather than a clash of ideas.

Here is communication as a meeting between two personalities who, whatever they gain by way of information in the process, discover more about each other as a result. This is the crucial distinction between two terms we tend to use interchangeably – information and communication. To *inform* is to exchange bits of news; to *communicate* is to disclose something of oneself in the act of passing on the bits of news.

So self-disclosure is at the heart of all true communication. But as Jacob discovered, God's self-disclosure is always veiled and mysterious. It is never without ambiguity. When his opponent leaves him, Jacob is still not *quite* sure with whom he has been dealing. 'Why do you want to know my name?' the stranger asks. Jacob believes he has met God and lived to tell the tale, but he doesn't know that beyond a shadow of a doubt. God slips away at dawn before he can be clearly seen in the morning light.

And it has turned out to be a painful and costly contest. Jacob emerges from the encounter with a pronounced limp, even though he has wrestled God to a draw. It's as though God were saying, 'By all means come up close, but only if you are prepared to pay the price.'

To state the obvious: the possibility of any form of Christian communication – whether through the mass media, the sermon, the printed word, in private conversation or prayer – is a pyramid upon a point: the assumption that God does not sit in heaven tight-lipped but is given to gracious acts of self-disclosure. And when there is true communication between God and the believer, what is passed on is not knowledge, however profound, but life; and not just life but divine life through Jesus Christ. The early Christians came to believe that Christ is the communicated self-expression of God.

Since God's purpose is to disclose something of himself, one way of looking at Christian doctrines is to see them as solutions to specific problems which might hinder that process.

Take the Trinity, which tackles head-on the question: how can a God whose nature is self-disclosure be solitary? God's social nature is part of his eternal being; it has never depended on his creatures providing him with companionship. Therefore, the urge to give, to share, to communicate, is the way the created order is meant to work because it reflects the inner nature of the Trinitarian God.

Another essential condition for true communication is equality. This is not to say there can only be real communication in a totally egalitarian society. Equality in the act of communication means the parties are willing, unconditionally, to give and to receive – they acknowledge their need of what the other has to offer. But how is this possible when the exchange is between an omnipotent God and a mortal creature? The answer of Christian doctrine is the Incarnation. As Calvin puts it, 'God bends down, and lowering himself, lisps into our ear that we might hear and understand.'

God confronts Jacob at the ford by the River Jabbok not as a pillar of fire nor as a blinding light but as a man. In what might be regarded as a dress rehearsal for the Incarnation, God seems to divest himself of divinity. The act of communication becomes an encounter between equals. The Incarnation is a levelling out of absolute inequalities for the purposes of communication. 'Christ,' says Paul, 'though he was rich became poor so that by his poverty we might become rich', or as St Ireneaus put it, 'He became what we are that we might become what he is.' In the radio business, this would be known as adjusting the frequencies so that voice and ear are on the same wavelength.

But self-disclosure involves all the risks of openness and vulnerability. To come out of the shadows is to present an inviting target. And if it is God who chooses to engage in self-disclosure, then he is the most inviting target of all. He who dwells in light unapproachable becomes the one who can be seen, heard and touched. And not all the hands laid on him were loving and respectful.

Which brings us to the cross as the inevitable price of God's self-disclosure. On Calvary, the very heart of God was nakedly exposed. The cross was perfect communication at infinite cost, shown by the theological word for Christ's saving work, atonement: personal relationship in total harmony without barrier or distance. And the proof text of atonement, 'God was in Christ reconciling the world to himself', is an image of parties coming into perfect alignment, all distortions being clarified.

Then again, a system of communication rather than a sporadic burst of messages passing hither and thither requires a network or grid with some degree of permanence. The Christian grid is the Communion of the Holy Spirit. In Bishop John V. Taylor's phrase, the distance between believers is bridged by the go-between God. The Holy Spirit powers the system. And the fruits of the Spirit – love, joy, peace and the rest – are precisely the qualities required to allow those who communicate to reveal themselves without fear of exploitation or manipulation.

Finally, when the gap between the parties is not just bridged but transcended then communication solidifies into communion. There is unity not just of meaning but of life: a new creation. The Bible is agnostic about the details of the unimaginable condition where the divine–human communication process is complete, when God has disclosed as much about himself as his creatures can bear. But it is a state described by terms such as *kabod* in the Old Testament and *doxa* in the New Testament: glory.

Jacob staggers away crippled from that wrestling match with God. He has paid the price for coming to grips with the divine. Admittedly, wrestling is an extreme form of touching and being touched, but it points forward to the method by which Jesus usually communicated physical and spiritual wholeness. When he was once asked, 'Who touched me?' it wasn't a complaint but an acknowledgement that the woman with the flux of blood had the right to do it. He risks ceremonial defilement to touch a leper; he squeezes the hand of Peter's sick mother-in-law; he lays his hand across the eyes of the two blind men, and touches the tongue of the deaf and dumb man at Decapolis – and so on and on.

Face-to-face contact was the original method of spreading the gospel. It is hard to think of more than a handful of instances where Jesus was beyond the reach of anyone who wished to tap him on the shoulder and ask him to honour the promises he made in his preaching.

Wrestling Jacob is a challenging image in the age of mass communication, where the pain and truth of personal encounter is easily lost. And it reminds us of the shocking particularity of Jesus' love which mocks *mass* media or *mass* anything. In John's Gospel he lifts his eyes to heaven and says, 'I do not pray for the *world* but for *these*', gesturing to those around him – not people *en masse*, but this individual and that one and the other.

At the heart of faith is always a face-to-face encounter, which as Jacob discovered, can be costly. According to Paul, the sign of true apostles is not that they are eloquent or wise but that they bear in their bodies the marks of the dying of the Lord Jesus: wounds obtained in close combat.

O that I knew where I might find him!

Job 23.3

Where shall I flee from your presence?

Psalm 139.7

There are those who deny God's reality and yet find something haunting about the idea. Bertrand Russell wrote of 'that which I do not find, do not think is to be found, but the love of it is my life'. Like the elusive Pimpernel, God is sought here, there and everywhere else without result.

And yet, though God is not to be found, the paradox is that he cannot be evaded either. The God who eludes us is also the God who haunts us. It is the same reality that Job longs to find and the psalmist seeks to evade. This baffling truth is at the heart of all true religion. Writes the US theologian John Knox, 'The fact is that we cannot really know God nor can we forget God. Though we cannot find him, we cannot escape him; though we cannot lay our hands on him, his hand will not let us go.'

In one of his books, A. N. Whitehead says that there are three stages in the true religious experience. Knowledge of God passes from the sense of God as void, to God as enemy, and then on to God as companion. These are not necessarily separate stages: the experiences may overlap. God the void signifies the futility of any search; God the enemy is our implacable pursuer who, when we capitulate to him, becomes our companion.

Thus the God we seek becomes the God who finds us. The God we try to evade possesses us. So our deepest needs are answered – the void is our emptiness aching to be filled; the enemy is our perpetual anxiety which needs to be allayed, and in our loneliness we cry out for a friend.

The Christian dares to put a name to the One who is both pursuer and evader. According to Jesus, he may be addressed as Father. It is a loving Father out on the road calling our name and urging us to come home. The great Jewish scholar C. G. Montefiore maintained that this was the one absolutely new thing that Jesus came to say. The idea of God inviting sinners back is not new, nor is that of God welcoming them back. But the idea of God seeking out sinners is quite new. A cosmic tyrant wouldn't do that; but a heavenly Father would and does.

Only once in the Bible is a father described as running. It is in the parable of the prodigal son. Perpetually, the father kept watch, and one evening there was something familiar about the walk of someone coming towards the house: 'When he was a great way off, the father saw him and ran . . .'

The Spirit of God was brooding on the face of the waters

Genesis 1.2

The biblical epic of creation depicts a scene of primeval chaos – darkness, mystery and formlessness. But above the ceaseless roar of clashing systems, the Artist-God pauses, pondering how and where he will apply the supreme creative energy of his love. The idea of a 'brooding' spirit makes permissible the image of the pensive artist, rubbing his chin, furrowing his brow and wrestling with the problems of form, structure and relationship. 'What shall I do with this? How shall I fashion that?' And like all true artistic impulses, the creative love of God is applied in silence. There is no noise and self-important flurry.

So we are taken behind the scenes, away from the vast stellar spaces and the explosions of energy to where God the thinker broods on his material, like a musician on a theme, until the moment of creation comes, then truth, life and beauty appear. God's perfect taste is brought to bear on the imperfect raw material of the universe; the Spirit draws out its latent possibilities, the beauty, wonder and variety of life.

God's love in history acts positively as creativity, giving form to the formless, inspiring beauty, significance and holiness, fashioning the kingdom of heaven out of chaos. But creation's work is still unfinished; the Artist-God works on in a co-operative endeavour – inspiring a new creation of which Christ is the focus. The Artist-God looks over our shoulder when we are unsure of our technique, just as the masters of classical painting guided the brush-strokes of their pupils. The label 'School of Tintoretto' meant that the great artist guaranteed the quality of the work done under his direction and added his own distinctive touches where appropriate. 'Perfected in love' would be a biblical way of describing God's distinctive touches to the efforts of those who have put themselves to school with him.

Evelyn Underhill wrote, 'The energy of Divine love will never do for us what we ought to do for ourselves; but will ever back up the creature's efforts by its grace, coming into action just as our action fails. This is the secret that has always been known to men and women of prayer; something we can trust and that acts in proportion to our trust.' The Spirit cleanses our will and purges our emotions of unreal attachments so that we may take our place in the eternal order, having found our due role.

Dorothy L. Sayers expanded this theme in her book, *The Mind of the Maker* by arguing that every human act of creation, as for example writing, is threefold: creative vision, the realization of this vision and the impact of that vision on others. By analogy she derived from this the way in which God as Trinity works in the world. First there is the creative idea, timeless, beholding the whole work complete at once, the end in the beginning; thus, the Father. Then there is the creative energy, begotten of that idea, incarnate in matter; this is the image of the Word. Third, there is the creative power, the meaning of the work calling out a response in those who will heed it: the Spirit. None of these is effective without the other two; but together they form the Trinity – the Artist-God, whose great work is the Creation.

You must not worship gods
you have made yourself

Micah 5.13

Human beings have been described as 'worshipping animals'. We must find someone or something to be the object of our ultimate allegiance, and if all else fails, we will manufacture our own gods. Some of the most potent gods of modern times are the products of human ingenuity or devilry – political gods such as nationalism, fascism, communism or even democracy; intellectual gods such as science or hedonism.

In the twentieth century, science offered mankind some impressive gods. In 1902, Henry Adams, the American writer, visited the Great Exposition in Paris and spent the summer watching the newly invented giant dynamo in the Champs de Mars. To him, it seemed like a symbol of divinity. He wrote, 'I began to feel the forty-foot dynamo as a moral force, much as the early Christians felt the cross. Before the end, one began to pray to it.'

The Bible warns that we tend to grow like the gods we have manufactured. Wrote the psalmist, 'Their idols are silver and gold, the work of men's hands. They have mouths but they speak not; eyes they have but see not, and they that make them have become like them.'

The prophets had a down-to-earth way of sorting out the gods. The test was performance. Which god could deliver? The true God was the one who kept his word, who could do what he promised. In a trial of strength, those gods which were the work of human hands were bound to fail because they could not be any cleverer than their makers. This disposed decisively of the question: who is made in whose image?

There is, however, a huge problem here. How can we human beings whose main contact with the world is through our senses avoid giving some shape and form to whatever we come to believe in? We don't just think in terms of abstract principles; we think in pictures. Take one of the gods of the philosophers, say Cosmic Essence. Close your eyes and imagine a Cosmic Essence – perhaps a gigantic scent bottle? Or the god of the

Platonists – the Absolute Unknown? What can come into your mind other than a total blank? And if something or someone is absolutely unknown, they may as well not exist. We can't think in abstract terms, we think in pictures.

So if we think about God at all, we really don't have much choice other than to become idolaters, because we are trying to get our minds around a reality that is strictly beyond human comprehension. For instance, in one Old Testament incident, God refuses to allow human beings to pin a label on him; he tells Moses 'Call me "I will be what I will be."' In other words, don't give me a name or you'll begin to visualize me, form an idol in your mind. Yet in the same book, Genesis, God is described as walking in the Garden of Eden; he stretches out his arm, his voice shakes the cedars, he can be tasted and found good. What is that but a picture, an image and therefore an idol? To forbid the making of pictures about God would be to rule out any thoughts of him at all. We need models, symbols, pictures to focus our minds and fire our imaginations.

If mental pictures of God are inevitable, by far the best and safest are those which are cast in the form of human personality and qualities – God as king, as father, as mother, as friend. Whatever is highest and best in human nature could form an impression of God provided we recognize its limitations and are aware of its dangers. Human personality is the highest form of existence known to us in creation, so that is inevitably the source of our pictures of God.

But we must recognize that even the human model, though a thousand miles removed from the crude idols of wood and stone, is still a form of idolatry. Jesus himself was always conscious of the danger of his followers turning him into an idol, which is why he commanded them to look beyond himself to his Father. According to the fourth Gospel, he warned his disciples, 'He who believes in me doesn't believe in me but in him who sent me.' And Paul looked to the time when God would be all in all, with even the Son in subjection to him.

The Society for Promoting Christian Knowledge (SPCK) was founded in 1698. Its mission statement is:

To promote Christian knowledge by

- **Communicating the Christian faith in its rich diversity;**
- **Helping people to understand the Christian faith and to develop their personal faith; and**
- **Equipping Christians for mission and ministry.**

SPCK Worldwide serves the Church through Christian literature and communication projects in over 100 countries, and provides books for those training for ministry in many parts of the developing world. This worldwide service depends upon the generosity of others and all gifts are spent wholly on ministry programmes, without deductions.

SPCK Bookshops support the life of the Christian community by making available a full range of Christian literature and other resources, providing support for those training for ministry, and assisting bookstalls and book agents throughout the UK.

SPCK Publishing produces Christian books and resources, covering a wide range of inspirational, pastoral, practical and academic subjects. Authors are drawn from many different Christian traditions, and publications aim to meet the needs of a wide variety of readers in the UK and throughout the world.

The Society does not necessarily endorse the individual views contained in its publications, but hopes they stimulate readers to think about and further develop their Christian faith.

For further information about the Society, visit our website at *www.spck.org.uk* or write to:
SPCK, 36 Causton Street,
London SW1P 4ST, United Kingdom.